I0002670

<u>Disclaimer</u>

The publisher of this book is by no way associated with the National Institute of Standards and Technology (NIST). The NIST did not publish this book. It was published by 50 page publications under the public domain license.

50 Page Publications.

Book Title: A Profile for IPv6 in the U.S. Government - Version 1.0

Book Author: Douglas C. Montgomery; J. S. Nightingale; Sheila E. Frankel; Mark E. Carson

Book Abstract: This publication seeks to assist Federal agencies in formulating plans for the acquisition of IPv6 technologies. To achieve this, we define a standards profile for IPv6 in the USG that is intended to be applicable to all future uses of IPv6 in non-classified, non-national security federal IT systems. The standards profile is meant to: (a) define a simple taxonomy of common network devices; (b)define their minimal mandatory IPv6 capabilities and identify significant configuration options so as to assist agencies in the development of more specific acquisition and deployment plans; and, (c) provide the technical basis upon which future USG polices can be defined.

Citation: NIST SP - 500-267

Keyword: Internet Protocol Version 6, IPv6, USGv6, Standards Profile

Special Publication 500-267

National Institute of
Standards and Technology
U.S. Department of Commerce

A Profile for IPv6 in the U.S. Government – Version 1.0

Recommendations of the National Institute of Standards and Technology

Doug Montgomery, Stephen Nightingale, Sheila Frankel and Mark Carson

NIST Special Publication 500-267

A Profile for IPv6 in the U.S. Government – Version 1.0

Recommendations of the National Institute of Standards and Technology

Doug Montgomery, Stephen Nightingale, Sheila Frankel and Mark Carson

---

Information Technology Laboratory

Attn: USGv6 Project
National Institute of Standards and Technology
Gaithersburg, MD 20899-8920
usgv6-project@antd.nist.gov

July 2008

U.S. Department of Commerce

Carlos M. Gutierrez, Secretary

National Institute of Standards and Technology

James M. Turner, Deputy Director

Reports on Computer Systems Technology

The Information Technology Laboratory (ITL) at the National Institute of Standards and Technology (NIST) promotes the U.S. economy and public welfare by providing technical leadership for the nation's measurement and standards infrastructure. ITL develops tests, test methods, reference data, proof of concept implementations, and technical analysis to advance the development and productive use of information technology. ITL's responsibilities include the development of technical, physical, administrative, and management standards and guidelines for the cost-effective security and privacy of sensitive unclassified information in Federal computer systems. This Special Publication 500-series reports on ITL's research, guidance, and outreach efforts in Information Technology and its collaborative activities with industry, government, and academic organizations.

National Institute of Standards and Technology Special Publication 500-267
NIST SP 500-267, 76 pages, (July 2008)

Acknowledgements

The authors would like to acknowledge the members of the Federal Government IPv6 Working Group for their keen and insightful assistance throughout the development of the document, and the members of the wider Federal Government who offered useful technical and editorial comments. During the investigation, development and initial review of this document, many people and organizations were consulted and offered technical and procedural insights. Of particular note are the more than 500 comments from more than 50 sources in Government and industry that we received during the two public comment periods on the earlier drafts. Continuing dialogue among members of the Federal IPv6 Working Group, in particular Pete Tseronis, Carol Bales, Kshemendra Paul and Roxie Murphy, has helped significantly to shape this technical profile, and several potential policy issues surrounding it.

This profile has undergone several iterations of harmonization with the DoD Standard Profiles for IPv6 Capable Products. We would like to acknowledge the fruitful input and discussions with the participants in the DISR IPv6 Standards Working Group, in particular: Ralph Liguori, Ed Jankiewicz, Jeremy Duncan and Kris Strance. Both profiling efforts have benefited from these exchanges.

Planning for the compliance testing program to support this profile benefited greatly from all the participants who attended two public workshops on the topic. In particular representatives of the IPv6Ready Logo program (Erica Johnson and Tim Winters), the Joint Interoperability Test Command (JITC) IPv6 test program (Jeremy Duncan), and the TAHI project (Hiroshi Miyata and Chih-Cheng Tsao), among others, helped us understand existing efforts and how they might be leveraged.

We also appreciate the invaluable assistance of colleagues here at NIST, including Tim Polk, William MacGregor, Gordon Gillerman, Darrin Santay, Joyce Malones, Karen Scarfone and Tim Grance, who reviewed drafts of this document and/or contributed to its technical content.

Table of Contents

List of Appendices

Executive Summary

The suite of protocols commonly known as Internet Protocol version 6 (IPv6) has been under design and development within the Internet Engineering Task Force (IETF) and the Internet industry for over 10 years [1]. This industry led effort was initiated in the early 1990's to address perceived scaling problems in the Internet's addressing and routing architectures. Today stable standards exist for basic IPv6 functionality. Commercial implementations and services based upon these specifications are emerging, and vendors and large user groups are pursuing significant product development and technology adoption plans for IPv6.

The United States Government (USG) is one such large user group, and most Agencies across the government are beginning to plan for the adoption and deployment of IPv6 technologies in response to: mission driven technical and economic assessments of the technology [161]; broad Government policies [166] [167] [170]; the product release plans of major vendors; and, the plans and actions of other organizations on the Internet.

Given the prevalence and importance of Internet technologies in Federal information technology (IT) systems today and the nature and scale of both the opportunities and risks associated with significant deployments of new networking technologies, NIST was tasked [166] with an effort to evaluate the need for additional standards and testing infrastructures to support USG plans for IPv6 adoption. As part of this effort we examined the state of IPv6 specifications published by the IETF; the present state of maturity of commercial implementations; the evolving Department of Defense IPv6 profile [152] and product testing program [153]; and, national and international profiles and testing programs driven by the vendor communities [151][176] [178]. The objective of this analysis was to determine: (a) where significant technical gaps exist in the near term technical landscape for IPv6 deployment; (b) what, if any, additional standards and testing infrastructures and processes are needed to assist Federal agencies to achieve safe and economical adoption of this new technology.

Our findings from these efforts include:

1. A subset of network layer IPv6 specifications has stabilized and operationally viable commercial implementations of these specifications are becoming available. Agency budgeting, procurement and deployment planning, could benefit from a common identification and definition of such IPv6 capabilities.

2. While significant commercial implementations have and continue to emerge, broad vendor product lines are currently at varying levels of maturity and completeness. Until there is time for significant market forces to effectively define *de facto* standard levels of completeness and correctness, product testing services are likely needed to ensure the confidence and to protect the investment of early IPv6 adopters.

3. The current state of IPv6 security and network protection technologies and operational knowledge lags behind that of IPv4 and the existing Internet. Additional efforts are required to "raise the bar" in these areas to ensure the safety of IPv6 deployments in operational Federal information technology systems.

4. While, in general, the proliferation of technology standards is to be avoided, the existing DoD and industry profiling and testing efforts are currently not well suited in content, or governance, for the perceived requirements of the USG as a whole. In the near term, the broad requirements of civilian agencies can be better met by a distinct profile and testing program. In the long term we are committed to the harmonization and convergence of these efforts into broader, international

collaborative user/vendor profiling and testing initiatives in which the technical and process requirements of the USG can be fully accommodated.

5. Some key IPv6 design issues remain unresolved. As the USG begins to undertake significant operational deployments and investments in IPv6 technology, additional efforts are warranted to ensure that the eventual resolution of these design issues remains consistent with USG requirements and investments.

This document recommends a technology acquisition profile for common IPv6 devices to be procured and deployed in operational USG IT systems. It is intended to address several aspects of findings 1, 3, 4 and 5 above and will be augmented by additional documents and activities including:

- Development of guidance for the secure deployment of IPv6 to further address findings 3 and 5.

- Development of an open public testing program for IPv6 technologies [160] to further address finding 2.

This standards profile is meant to: (a) define a simple taxonomy of common network devices; (b) define their minimal mandatory IPv6 capabilities and identify significant configuration options so as to assist agencies in the development of more specific acquisition and deployment plans; and, (c) provide the technical basis upon which future USG polices can be defined. The scope of the device taxonomy and the selection of mandatory capabilities and identified options are purposefully conservative in some ways; defining systems and capabilities that are thought to be of common utility to the USG as a whole. In other ways, this profile "raises the bar" for some areas of IPv6 technology that are thought vital to protect the current and future security of Federal IT systems and to protect the economic investment of early adopters.

The profile and associated test program will provide the technical basis for the definition and demonstration of "IPv6 Capable" and "IPv6 Compliant" for USG procurements. The profile is forward looking and as such we recommend that users and vendors be given 24 months after publication of the latest version to respond to any new technical requirements.

Note that it is fully expected that agencies would further augment and/or modify these specifications to meet the requirements of specific IT system procurements and policies. In particular, the profile defines certain significant configuration choices that must be made and specified to fully articulate the set of mandatory requirements for each class and/or instance of device.

1. Introduction

This profile has been prepared for use by Federal agencies. It can be used by other organizations on a voluntary basis and is not subject to copyright. If used in other (non-USG) contexts, accurate attribution/citation is desired so as to avoid confusion.

Nothing in this document is intended to contradict standards and guidelines made mandatory and binding on Federal agencies by the Secretary of Commerce under statutory authority, nor ought this profile to be interpreted as altering or superseding the existing authorities of the Secretary of Commerce, Director of the Office of Management and Budget, or any other Federal official.

1.1 Purpose and Scope

This publication seeks to assist Federal agencies in formulating plans for the acquisition of IPv6 technologies. To achieve this, we define a standards profile for IPv6 in the USG that is intended to be applicable to all future uses of IPv6 in non-classified, non-national security [157] federal IT systems. The standards profile is meant to: (a) define a simple taxonomy of common network devices; (b) define their minimal mandatory IPv6 capabilities and identify significant configuration options so as to assist agencies in the development of more specific acquisition and deployment plans; and, (c) provide the technical basis upon which future USG polices can be defined. A profile in this context is a compendium of protocol specifications, with normativity statements (MUST, SHOULD, MAY, etc) highlighted or strengthened. Most specifications identified are published by the IETF, though USG, DoD, IEEE, ISO/IEC and other organizations publications are not precluded. Common use of the word *specification* in this profile implies no particular publisher.

The profile is meant to be a landmark to guide the acquisition of significant new IPv6 capabilities for operational Federal IT systems. No attempt has been made to grandfather existing early implementations, or cover potential non-production level uses of the technology in test-beds, pilots, etc. In summary, the profile is meant as a strategic planning guide for future acquisitions and as such appropriate lead times must be allowed between its publication and its use in procurements. Other uses of this profile, without agency specific refinement, are not recommended. In particular, this acquisition profile should not be thought of as a deployment or transition guide or as suggesting operational requirements for USG networks. Guidance and policies covering these other, post acquisition, issues are outside the scope of this profile.

The scope of the device taxonomy and the selection of mandatory capabilities and identified options are purposefully conservative in some ways; defining systems and capabilities that are thought to be of common utility to the USG as a whole. In other ways, this profile "raises the bar" for some areas of IPv6 technology that are thought vital to protect the current and future security of Federal IT systems and to protect the economic investment of early adopters.

It is fully expected that agencies will further augment and/or modify these specifications to meet their own requirements when making IT system specifications and policies. To assist in such a process, this profile defines a number of configuration options that a user (e.g., acquisition authority) must specify to fully articulate the IPv6 capability requirements of specific procurements. But, beyond selection among configuration options, agencies with specific mission requirements might substantially modify the conformance requirements of the technical profile. Where this is done, care needs to be taken to insure that systems that meet the new, derivative requirements remain interoperable with systems that conform to this profile.

1.2 Audience

This document is intended to assist several communities of interest in the strategic planning and implementation of IPv6 adoption programs within the USG. Potential uses of this profile range from establishing a technical basis for USG-wide acquisition policies, to providing guidance for individual procurement actions. Equally important, this document acts as a statement of strategic IPv6 technical direction for a large IT user group (the USG) and as a potential vehicle for communication to a broad product industry.

This profile assumes that the users have some level of familiarity with both the base capabilities and technologies of IPv6 and with its corpus of specifications (i.e. IETF RFCs). The technical specification of capabilities required by modern networking devices is inherently complex. While some use the term "IPv6" as if it were a single, monolithic technology with a simple concise technical definition, the reality is quite different. The complete specification of viable IPv6-capabilities requires reference to hundreds of individual protocol, architecture, and algorithm specifications. While this profile provides some background and rationale about the choices that are contained within it, it is well beyond the scope of this document to provide a tutorial on these technologies and specifications. Readers are directed to the wealth of books and training materials that provide such introductions to IPv6 technologies.

The main purpose of this document is to identify and organize the vast collection of IPv6 specifications into subsets of mandatory and conditional requirements that may be of common utility in planning for and acquiring specific IPv6 products and services. As such, the profile is primarily targeted to users in the following groups:

- **Contracts and Acquisition** - Acquisition officers and others writing purchasing and contract language may use this document as a reference when they develop specific product and system requirement text. For their purposes, this document aims to adequately summarize the IPv6 technical requirements that must be met for products to be considered *USGv6-V1-Capable* in general and *USGv6-V1-Compliant* to a specific product/system definition. It should be noted that this profile only addresses IPv6 requirements, and thus cannot stand in isolation as a complete procurement specification. Many other technical issues (e.g., IPv4 capabilities, hardware, performance, reliability, support) and procurement regulations must be typically addressed and specified to fully define a complete procurement requirement.
- **Testing and Accreditation Organizations** – In Section 7, this profile outlines the plan for testing and documenting compliance to the specified requirements. The USGv6 test program will rely upon accredited laboratories executing standardized test procedures and methods. This profile provides the target, and thus starting point, for the further definition of the test program. As such, the profile will be of direct interest to test laboratories, accreditation bodies, and test equipment/systems vendors.
- **Developers** – Developers of Host, Routers and Network Protection Devices and software should view this document as a statement of direction and intent for the USG IT networking marketplace. As such, the IPv6 technical requirements contained within the profile are expected to be implemented by significant numbers of this community.
- **System Designers / Integrators** - The engineers and managers responsible for systems development within the USG should look to this document as a strategic guide as to the networking capabilities to be expected in future networked systems. As such, they should consider how to use these capabilities in their broader systems-level designs, and should review these capabilities for gaps considered crucial to future systems requirements.

All members of this audience, and others, are encouraged to carefully review this profile and provide comments so that future versions might be improved. Comments should be addressed to:
sp500-267-comments@antd.nist.gov.

1.3   Profile Structure and Conventions

The remainder of this document is organized into seven major sections and several supporting appendices. Section 2 on Architectural Issues discusses broad considerations and choices of IPv6 related protocols as they affect Federal Intranet and Internet infrastructure. Sections 3, 4, and 5 provide configuration templates for three classes of devices addressed by this profile. Section 6 provides motivation and interpretation of the precise sets of IPv6 technical requirements that are specified in the normative requirements table in section 8. Finally, section 7 outlines the plan for the testing and documentation requirements necessary for devices to demonstrate compliance with these requirements. Two appendices provide lists of the references and terms employed throughout the document.

1.3.1   Statements of Requirement Levels

The terminology used to describe requirements levels in this profile include: "mandatory", "optional" (with their common meaning), and "MUST", "MUST NOT", "REQUIRED", "SHALL", "SHALL NOT", "SHOULD", "SHOULD NOT", "RECOMMENDED", "MAY", and "OPTIONAL" which are to be interpreted as described in [RFC2119]. In addition, this profile adopts the use of the term "SHOULD+"to indicate a requirement that is equivalent to "SHOULD" in this version of this specification, but is expected to be elevated to a "MUST" in future versions (see section 1.4 on Profile Life Cycles).

Note that this profile places no requirements or constraints on technologies, capabilities or functions that are not explicitly listed in this document. That is, all IPv6 capabilities not mentioned in the profile should be considered as optional, or MAY (as long as support of such features do not affect conformance to a mandatory requirement of the profile). Another way of thinking about this is that specification of function that is unconditionally marked as optional/MAY in our profile, could have been completely omitted from the specification, without changing the normative requirements. In a few places we include references and requirements that are marked unconditionally as optional. We only do so to (1) override a more stringent requirement in the base specification, (2) highlight a choice that we feel others might want to reconsider, or (3) for the sake of clarity or consistency with other requirements.

1.3.2   Taxonomy of Device Types

In specifying capability requirements for devices it is necessary to recognize that different types of devices play different roles in many protocol specifications. The IETF defines an *IPv6 Node* as a device that implements IPv6. The IETF IPv6 specifications recognize two types of Nodes, *Hosts* and *Routers*. *IPv6 Node Requirements* [RFC4294] expresses a general profile of device requirements in terms of these two device types. We adopt and maintain this taxonomy of device types in this profile. In addition, our profile defines requirements for *Network Protection Devices (NPDs)*, which often have only partial, or non-standard, Host and/or Router capabilities. For this reason, and because this profile only specifies the protection capabilities required for these devices, we call them out as a distinct device type.

When a specification that distinguishes Host and Router behaviors is cited for a device type in this profile, we implicitly mean that the required Host behavior applies to our Host device type and the required Router behavior applies to our Router device type. Put another way, a device claiming to conform to the Host requirements of this profile, must implement the Host behaviors (when distinguished) in the referenced specifications. Similarly, a device claiming to conform to the Router requirements of this profile, must implement the Router behaviors (when distinguished) in the referenced specifications.

It should be noted that we use these notions of device types to identify and group sets of requirements into collections that correspond to these two basic architectural roles. Such a typology is representative of specifications not implementations. Where specifications classify required behaviors along different taxonomies (e.g. client/server, initiator/responder, etc) we will explicitly reference these identified roles in our requirements. It is understood that any combination of device types can be implemented together 'in one box'. Thus a Host and a NPD (e.g., Firewall) could be bundled together, for example.

In summary, there are three types of devices in this profile: Hosts, Routers and Network Protection Devices, defined as:

- **Host:** any Node that is not a Router. A Host's primary purpose is to support application protocols that are the source and/or destination of IP layer communication.

- **Router:** a Node that interconnects sub-networks by packet forwarding. A Router's primary purpose is to support the control protocols necessary to enable interconnection of distinct IP sub-networks by IP layer packet forwarding.

- **Network Protection Device:** Firewalls or Intrusion Detection / Prevention devices that examine and selectively block or modify network traffic.

It is our belief that the vast majority of devices that this profile can and will be applied too, fit within this simple taxonomy. The configuration options that exist in each device category allow for a selective range of requirements to be chosen on a per use, per device basis. These configuration options effectively allow profile users to instantiate sets of capability requirements that correspond to more specific *product classes* within a given device type. Where such options do not exist, we feel that the required functionality is important to establish as the ubiquitous interoperability base for future USG use, and that allowing a proliferation of partial subsets of these capabilities is not desirable.

While certain common classes of current products, or certain current deployment scenarios, might suggest further partitioning of the device taxonomy, we feel that would have diminishing value and possibly detrimental effects in such a broad document as this. The base standards only define behavior and requirements in the simple terms of Host/Router, Client/Server, etc. The further classification of requirements into specific product classes seems somewhat subjective. Rather, this specificity can be achieved in a more flexible fashion through the configuration options provided in this profile. For example, using the configuration options provided with the Host device type, a user of the profile can further articulate the requirements that would distinguish a typical personal computer, scientific workstations, network server, etc. Using the configuration options provided with the Router device type, a user of the profile could further articulate the requirements that would distinguish a typical campus router from an Internet border gateway, etc.

Having said that, we realize that the range of networked IT devices is vast (e.g., Hosts range from super computers, to systems on a chip) and that some devices might have real mission and design requirements that can't be met by our device taxonomy and configuration options. As noted in the Purpose and Scope section, we fully expect that some USG requirements for IPv6 products cannot be met without modification of the requirements in this profile.

1.3.3 Functional Categories of IPv6 Capabilities

In order to provide some structure to the description and selection of IPv6 requirements, this profile defines several functional categories of capabilities. This taxonomy of capabilities and requirements is solely for the purpose of providing some modularity to our descriptions. The normative status of the requirements is not affected by which category they are documented in.

Each category is comprised of references to one or more specific technical specifications (mainly Internet Engineering Task Force (IETF) Request for Comments[1] (RFCs)). The requirements of this profile are defined by indicating specific conformance requirements to the individual specifications in their entirety and/or specific sub clauses. When we indicate a requirement level (e.g., mandatory/"M") for an entire specification, we are indicating the requirement to adhere to the normative clauses and explicit requirement levels within that specification. That is we are indicating the requirement to conform to the mandatory requirements of IETF specification, nothing more, nothing less. If it is felt that there is a need to override specific normative requirements within the specification, we will call out specific clauses and specify additional requirement levels for those clauses in this profile. Note that we sometimes do this just for emphasis or clarification, without changing the requirement level of the base specification.

Where we denote entire functional categories as "M" (mandatory) or "O" (optional), this denotes whether there are unconditional MUSTs within the category. Those functional categories labeled "M" have unconditional MUSTs in them and thus are applicable regardless of choices of configuration options. Those labeled "O" do not contain unconditional MUSTs and thus, for a given selection of configuration options, may not apply in a given instantiation of a fully specified set of requirements.

1.3.4 Individual Device Profiles

The IPv6 requirements for a given device type is comprised of an unconditional mandatory set, and sets of requirements that are conditional on various configuration options. Users of this profile must choose from the set of configuration options to complete the operative definition of a set of mandatory requirements. Some configuration options are effectively isolated Yes (include) or No (exclude) decisions about a set of requirements. Some configuration options are effectively a choice among alternatives, where one or more selections must be made. Such selection alternatives are labeled "O:n" which means: Optional, but you must choose at least n from this set.

Given a set of selections from the configuration options, the *USGv6-V1 Node Requirements Table (NRT)* in Section 8 prescribes the normative requirement set for that specific configuration instance.

Configuration options for Host, Routers and NPDs are made independently, and a common use of this profile might employ multiple instances of distinct Host requirements for distinct sets of required system capabilities embodied in a single procurement (e.g., PCs, workstations, servers). We caution users to use care in the selection of configuration options. The selection of major additional capabilities brings many issues of cost, complexity, availability and security with them. Some options provided in this profile are not commonly found in today's network environments (e.g., use of SNMP to manage Hosts) and as a result, probably not widely implemented. Users of this profile should carefully plan the IPv6 capabilities required for their future acquisitions, interact with the vendor community to understand the state of the marketplace for each capability, interact with the testing community to understand the state of the technology for each capability, and then, and only then, make their selections of required configuration options.

We use the label "USGv6-V1-Capable" for systems that conforms to the set of requirements that are unconditionally mandatory in the profile. A complete specification of requirements includes this set, plus the requirements that are mandatory under each of the selected configuration options. We use the label "USGv6-V1-Compliant" for systems that conform to such complete requirements specifications.

---

[1] Despite the connotation one might have of a "Request for Comments", IETF formal standards are published as RFCs.

1.3.5 Node Requirements Table

The definitive specification of the technical requirements of this profile is captured in the USGv6-V1 Node Requirements Table (NRT), in Section 8. The NRT provides a concise specification of the required IPv6 capabilities for each identified device type. Where the text descriptions in sections 3, 4, 5 and 6 of this document conflict with Section 8, or where they fail to specify functionality, the NRT in Section 8 takes precedence.

1.3.6 Additional Requirements

Clearly, if users require support of any capability that is left optional (e.g., MAY, SHOULD, SHOULD+) in a fully specified configuration, then they would have to document those modifications to the normative requirements of this profile. It should be equally clear, that this profile is limited only to specifying the requirements for IPv6 capabilities. In particular, it does not address the other details and requirements of IPv4-based protocols, nor many features of protocols that are not directly related to the support of IPv6. Thus, while this profile defines IPv6 capability requirements, it is not sufficient to fully specify the general procurement requirements for an actual product. Many details of hardware, software, additional protocol requirements, performance, reliability, support etc would have to augment these IPv6 requirement definitions, to result in a viable procurement specification of an actual device.

1.4 Profile Life Cycles and Change Management

The profile embodied in this document is a strategic planning tool for procurement officials, IPv6 product suppliers, testing laboratories, test product suppliers and laboratory accreditation bodies. One implication of developing a forward looking profile is that it is unreasonable to expect the product and testing industry to be able to respond immediately to new mandatory requirements as soon as they are published. Likewise, users and procurement officials need adequate time to plan for the acquisition and deployment of new capabilities.

As a general principle, we recommend that users and the product industry be given 24 months between the addition of a significant new mandatory requirement and citations of those requirements in procurement actions. Addition of new mandatory requirements that are viewed as incremental (e.g., minor revisions, extensions to existing mandatory requirements) should allow at least 12 months before being required in procurements. To capture these timing issues, each mandatory requirement specified in section 8 has an *Effective Date*, which reflects the principles above. The effective date of each mandatory requirement is earliest date that we recommend buyers asking for demonstrated compliance to a particular requirement.

In the future, we plan to issue a new version of this profile at most once per year. We consider the marking of a requirement as SHOULD+ (S+) as the indication of the intent to strengthen the requirement to MUST (M) in a future version of the profile. As a general principle, in future revisions of the profile, no significant new requirement will be made mandatory, that was not indicated as SHOULD+ in the previous version. Thus, going forward, significant new mandatory requirements will typically have at least 36 months lead time from the final publication of a profile version that flags the requirement with a SHOULD+ and the effective date that profile users should require demonstrated compliance with the requirement.

New mandatory requirements (e.g., maintenance revision to base standard already cited as a MUST) that are viewed as incremental may not follow the progression from SHOULD+ to MUST. In either case, such new incremental requirements will have an effective date of at least 12 months after the final publication of the profile version in which they are first included.

Profile users that modify/augment the mandatory requirements of this document for specific procurements should adhere to similar principles in the timing of their expectations of compliance and should clearly indicate an effective date for any new mandatory requirements.

As products and profiles evolve, the issues of compliance life cycle management can grow complex. In general, as new versions of the profile emerge, we recommend that users cite the most recent version of this profile. The details of how profile evolution and product evolution affect the validity of test results are issues that must be fully addressed in the detailed specification of the management plan for the test program. In general it is the objective of this test program to avoid gratuitous retesting of products where product enhancements or profile changes should not materially affect previous test results.

2. Architectural Issues

As agencies begin to adopt IPv6 technologies, they will need to establish a common interoperability strategy across the entire USG. While interoperability is important, it is also important that, for the sake of flexibility in adapting to individual agency's needs, the requirements intended to assure such interoperability not be over determined. Similarly, it is essential throughout the IPv6 adoption process, as new technologies are introduced, that each agency's infrastructure be continually protected. There are a number of ramifications to be explored here, some of which have in particular motivated the selection of specific device IPv6 capabilities in this profile.

Serious planning for IPv6 adoption in existing, or planned, IT systems is a very complex undertaking. The issues range from incremental deployment plans for new IPv6 data and control plane protocols, to coexistence and interoperation plans for existing IPv4 based infrastructure, to security and management plans for the resulting IPv6 (and mixed IPv4) infrastructure. Certainly a key factor in planning for IPv6 is the extent to which it must coexist and interoperate with an existing IPv4 infrastructure. It is beyond the scope of this profile to go into all the issues that must be considered; instead we provide reference to the following documents that address many of these issues in specific deployment and transition scenarios:

- **Enterprise Networks**:
    - o [RFC4057] *IPv6 Enterprise Network Scenarios.*
    - o [RFC4852] *IPv6 Enterprise Network Analysis - IP Layer 3 Focus.*
    - o [RFC3750] *Unmanaged Networks IPv6 Transition Scenarios.*
    - o [RFC3904] *Evaluation of IPv6 Transition Mechanisms for Unmanaged Networks.*
- **ISPs and Transit Network Infrastructure**:
    - o [RFC4029] *Scenarios and Analysis for Introducing IPv6 into ISP Networks.*
    - o [RFC2185] *Routing Aspects of IPv6 Transition.*
- **Interoperation with IPv4 Infrastructure**:
    - o [RFC4038] *Application Aspects of IPv6 Transition.*
    - o [RFC4213] *Basic Transition Mechanisms for IPv6 Hosts and Routers.*
- **Security Issues:**
    - o [RFC4942] *IPv6 Transition/Co-existence Security Considerations.*
    - o [RFC4864] *Local Network Protection for IPv6.*

Notwithstanding the issues outlined above, this profile assumes that the user's purpose is the planning and acquisition of IPv6 infrastructure for the establishment of widespread, eventually ubiquitous, deployment. The first step towards the successful adoption and widespread use of IPv6 is the establishment of a core network infrastructure[2] capable of providing IPv6 data services to the applications that will eventually follow. This profile addresses the devices and capabilities necessary to develop operationally viable IPv6 network services. In particular, this version of the profile primarily focuses on the network layer; specifying the minimal required IPv6 capabilities necessary for production level data-plane services that can operate at potentially large scales.

The key to IPv6 adoption in core network infrastructures resides in the capabilities of routers and their control (routing) protocols. This profile provides the minimal mandatory definition of an IPv6 Router. It distinguishes two sets of router device requirements, for interior gateways and exterior gateways.

---

[2] Our use of the term "core network infrastructure" refers to layer 3 data plane functions and should not be construed as having particular topological implications (e.g., backbones, edges, enterprise, distribution network segments).

Establishing an IPv6 core network infrastructure opens the door to creating new host applications adapted to exploit the added capabilities of the new infrastructure. It is exactly this potential, to develop new applications, at larger scales, that is the real, long term promise of IPv6. This profile provides the minimal mandatory definition of an IPv6 Host. The basic host IPv6 capabilities defined here provide the basis for building future applications. While it seems premature at this time to define the requirements of specific IPv6 applications, we offer guidance to the users of this profile that can be used to develop supplemental application requirements.

This is a profile for IPv6 technologies; it places no general requirements on the capabilities or uses of IPv4 technologies within the USG, other than addressing how the IPv6 systems can coexist and interoperate with existing IPv4 systems. These IPv4-IPv6 transition mechanisms are a vital element of most IPv6 deployment plans. Choosing a small, common set of mandatory transition mechanisms that can be easily managed and protected seems vital to insuring successful adoption and coexistence of IPv6 in the near to mid-term. This profile identifies dual-stack and tunneling mechanisms described in [RFC4213], as the basis for IPv4/IPv6 coexistence.

The Internet is not the safe academic space it was during the initial development of IPv4 in the 1970s and early 1980s. With the rise of dangers such as viruses, worms and denial of service attacks, network security technologies have become paramount in ensuring the viability and trustworthiness of networked IT systems. These technologies can be thought of in two groups: (1) IP security (IPsec) technologies designed to protect the trustworthiness and privacy of wanted communications, and (2) Network Protection Devices (NPDs) designed to detect and block unwanted communications.

- IPsec technologies are defined by the current compendium specification *Security Architecture for the Internet Protocol* [RFC4301], referred to in this document as *IPsec-v3*[3], which identifies encryption, authentication, integrity and secure transport mechanisms. IPsec is undergoing generational changes and while some existing implementations are based on the obsolete [RFC2401] architecture, referred to in this document as *IPsec-v2*, implementations of RFC4301 should be readily available by the effective date of this profile. We specify a security profile based on the "new IPsec" architecture and corresponding versions of the protocols for its implementation. The cryptographic algorithms specified are consistent with the new architecture and with other USG encryption policies.

- Although the IPv4 device industry is replete with Firewalls and Intrusion Detection Systems (IDSs), guidance documents, test specifications and even test and certification programs, an actual consensus specification for such devices seems to be absent. For this reason, this profile contains a specification for IPv6-enabled *Network Protection Devices* in section 6.12.

In sum, this profile is a reasoned selection of specifications, mostly RFCs, grouped into functional categories and configuration options that can be used to enumerate sets of specific product requirements for individual procurements.

---

[3] There are no generally accepted names for *IPsec-v3* and *IPsec-v2*; these terms are used in the document to make the requirements more understandable.

3.   Host Profile

This section outlines the IPv6 requirements for Host devices. The USGv6-V1 Node Requirements Table in Section 8 fully articulates the detailed normative requirements for a given selection of Host configuration options, while section 6 provides related discussion and interpretation. Please see the section 1.3.4 for a general discussion of the method and meaning of fully specifying the IPv6 requirements for a specific Host device configuration. A template of the various Host requirement sets and configuration options are given below along with references to sections of this profile that provide further discussion and interpretation of the requirements.

USGv6-V1 Host Requirements Template:
- [M] – **IPv6 Basic Requirements** – see section 6.1.
    - [O:1] – **SLAAC** – require support of stateless address auto-configuration.
    - [O:1] – **DHCP-Client** – require support of stateful (DHCP) address auto-configuration.
    - [Y/N] – **PrivAddr** – require support of SLAAC privacy extensions.
    - [Y/N] – **SEND** – require support of neighbor discovery security extensions.
- [M] – **Addressing Requirements** – see section 6.6.
    - [Y/N] – **CGA** – require support of cryptographically generated addresses.
- [O] – **Application Requirements** – see section 6.11.
    - [Y/N] – **DNS-Client** – require support of DNS client/resolver functions.
    - [Y/N] – **SOCK** – require support of Socket application program interfaces.
    - [Y/N] – **URI** – require support of IPv6 uniform resource identifiers.
    - [Y/N] – **DNS-Server** – require support of a DNS server application.
    - [Y/N] – **DHCP-Server** – require support of a DHCP server application.
- [M] – **IP Security Requirements** – see section 6.7.
    - [M] – **IPsec-V3** – require support of the IP security architecture.
    - [M] – **IKEv2** – require support for automated key management.
    - [M] – **ESP** – require support for encapsulating security payloads in IP.
- [O] – **Transition Mechanism Requirements** – see section 6.4.
    - [Y/N] – **IPv4** – require support to enable interoperation with IPv4-only systems.
- [O] – **Network Management Requirements** – see section 6.8.
    - [Y/N] – **SNMP** – require support of network management services.
- [M] – **Multicast Requirements** – see section 6.9.
    - [Y/N] – **SSM** – require full support of multicast communications.
- [O] – **Mobility Requirements** – see section 6.10.
    - [Y/N] – **MIP** – require support of capability for this host to be a mobile node.
- [O] – **Quality of Service Requirements** – see section 6.3.
    - [Y/N] – **DS** – require support of Differentiated Services capabilities.
- [M] – **Link Specific Technologies** – see section 6.5.
    - [O:1] – **Link** – require support of 1 or more link technologies.
    - [Y/N] – **ROHC** – require support of robust packet compression services.

We use the shorthand notation below to describe such complete configurations. For example a specification for nine fixed Hosts plus three mobile Hosts might look as follows:
- 9 hosts compliant[4] to: USGv6-V1-Capable+DHCP-client+Sock+DNS-Client+Link=Ethernet
- 3 hosts compliant to: USGv6-V1-Capable+SLAAC+Sock+DNS-Client+MIP+Link=PPP+Link=Ethernet

---

[4] See section 7 for a discussion of the meaning of compliance.

4. Router Profile

This section outlines the IPv6 requirements for Router devices. The USGv6-V1 Node Requirements Table in Section 8 fully articulates the detailed technical requirements, while section 6 provides related discussion and interpretation. Please see the section 1.3.4 for a general discussion of the method and meaning of fully specifying the IPv6 requirements for a specific Router device configuration. A template of the various Router requirement sets and configuration options are given below along with references to sections of this profile that provide further discussion and interpretation of the requirements. A template of the various Router requirement sets and configuration options are given below along with references to sections of this profile that provide further discussion and interpretation of the requirements.

USGv6-V1 Router Requirements Template:
- [M] – **IPv6 Basic Requirements** – see section 6.1.
  - [Y/N] – **DHCP-Client** – require support of stateful (DHCP) address auto-configuration.
  - [Y/N] – **DHCP-Prefix** – require support of automated router prefix delegation.
  - [Y/N] – **SEND** – require support of neighbor discovery security extensions.
- [M] – **Addressing Requirements** – see section 6.6.
  - [Y/N] – **CGA** – require support of cryptographically generated addresses.
- [O] – **Application Requirements** – see section 6.11.
  - [Y/N] – **DNS-Client** – require support of DNS client/resolver functions.
  - [Y/N] – **URI** – require support of IPv6 uniform resource identifiers.
  - [Y/N] – **DNS-Server** – require support of a DNS server application.
  - [Y/N] – **DHCP-Server** – require support of a DHCP server application.
- [O] – **Routing Protocol Requirements** – see section 6.2.
  - [Y/N] – **IGW** – require support of the intra-domain (interior) routing protocols.
  - [Y/N] – **EGW** – require support for inter-domain (exterior) routing protocols.
- [M] – **IP Security Requirements** – see section 6.7.
  - [M] – **IPsec-V3** – require support of the IP security architecture.
  - [M] – **IKEv2** – require support for automated key management.
  - [M] – **ESP** – require support for encapsulating security payloads in IP.
- [O] – **Transition Mechanism Requirements** – see section 6.4.
  - [Y/N] – **IPv4** – require support to enable interoperation with IPv4-only systems.
  - [Y/N] – **6PE** – require support of tunneling IPv6 over IPv4 MPLS services.
- [M] – **Network Management Requirements** – see section 6.8.
  - [M] – **SNMP** – require support of network management services.
- [M] – **Multicast Requirements** – see section 6.9.
  - [Y/N] – **SSM** – require full support of multicast routing services.
- [O] – **Mobility Requirements** – see section 6.10.
  - [Y/N] – **MIP** – require support of mobile IP home agent capabilities.
  - [Y/N] – **NEMO** – require support of mobile network capabilities.
- [M] – **Quality of Service Requirements** – see section 6.3.
  - [M] – **DS** – require support of Differentiated Services capabilities.
- [M] – **Link Specific Technologies** – see section 6.5.
  - [O:1] – **Link** – require support of 1 or more link technologies.
  - [Y/N] – **ROHC** – require support of robust packet compression services.

An example specification of an instance of Router requirements is:

- 5 routers compliant to: USGv6-V1-Capable+DHCP-Prefix+EGW+IPv4+6PE+SSM+Link=MAPOS

5. Network Protection Device Profile

This section outlines the IPv6 requirements for Network Protection Devices (NPD). The USGv6-V1 Node Requirements Table in section 8 fully articulates the detailed technical requirements, while section 6 provides related discussion and interpretation. Please see the Section 1.3.4 for a general discussion of the method and meaning of fully specifying the IPv6 requirements for a specific NPD device configuration. A template of the various NPD requirement sets and configuration options are given below along with references to sections of this profile that provide further discussion and interpretation of the requirements.

USGv6-V1 NPD Requirements Template:
- [M] – **Network Protection Device Requirements** – see section 6.12.
    - o   [O:1] – **FW** – require support of basic firewall capabilities.
    - o   [O:1] – **APFW** – require support of application firewall capabilities.
    - o   [O:1] – **IDS** – require support of intrusion detection capabilities.
    - o   [O:1] – **IPS** – require support of intrusion protection capabilities.

Network protection devices can effectively operate as either routers or hosts, with respect to network traffic flow. However, given their specialized functionality, they are not normally expected to operate as fully compliant general-purpose nodes. In fact, some classes of network protection devices are deployed in combination with general-purpose routers and hosts to affect a desired security architecture.

Rather than attempt to characterize the entire range of such potential combined or variant devices, we instead focus on the specialized security functionality that differentiates network protection devices from typical hosts and routers. These specialized requirements are discussed in Subsection 6.12 and listed in Section 8.

Clearly providing network protection services in IPv6 networks requires at least partial support for many IPv6 specifications (e.g., ability to parse IPv6 packets, support IPv6 addressing, encapsulate IPv6 on specific Link technologies, etc). Some network protection devices may even provide full Host or Router functionality. In such cases, users may require that such augmented devices also meet the full requirements of the corresponding device profiles. Any requirements for IPv6 capabilities beyond those defined in subsection 6.12 are the responsibility of the user to specify.

We use the shorthand notation USGv6-V1-NPD to summarize the unconditional mandatory requirements of NPDs and the same "+ notation" to denoted the selected configuration options in a fully specified set for requirements. An example specification of an instance of NPD requirements is:
- 2 firewalls compliant to: USGv6-V1-NPD+APFW+IDS

6.   Functional Categories of IPv6 Capabilities

This section provides informative explanation and clarification of the normative requirements specified in USGv6-V1 Node Requirements Table in section 8. In order to provide some structure to the lengthy description of IPv6 requirements, this profile defines several functional categories of IPv6 capabilities (see Section 1.3.3 for further discussion of this taxonomy). The table below identifies the categories and examples of the technologies addressed in each.

Table 1 - Functional Categories of IPv6 Capabilities

Section	Functional Category	Notes - Examples
6.1	IPv6 Basic Capabilities	IPv6, ND, SLAAC, DHCP
6.2	Routing Protocols	OSPF, BGP
6.3	Quality of Service	DiffServ
6.4	Transition Mechanisms	Dual Stack, Tunneling, 6PE
6.5	Link Specific	IP over X, ROHC
6.6	Addressing	IPv6 global, ULA, CGA
6.7	IP Security	IPsec, IKE, ESP, Crypto Algos
6.8	Network Management	SNMP, MIBs
6.9	Multicast	MLDV, PIM-SM
6.10	Mobility	MIP, Nemo
6.11	Application Requirements	Sockets, DNS, URIs, guidance.
6.12	Network Protection Device Requirements	Firewalls, intrusion detection systems.

The definitive normative requirements in each of these categories are specified in the Node Requirements Table in section 8. The subsections that follow provide informative discussion of the motivation for those requirements and additional information for clarification. Where there might be discrepancies between these subsections that follow and the Node Requirements Table in section 8, the table takes precedence.

6.1 IPv6 Basic Capabilities

The normative definition of technical requirements for this category is contained in the IPv6 Basic Requirements section of the USGv6-V1 Node Requirements Table in section 8. This section of the document provides informative discussion of the motivation for those requirements and additional information for clarification.

We include in the IPv6 Basic Requirements category those protocols and capabilities that are inherently tied to the fundamental operation and configuration of the Internet Protocol (IP) layer. For IPv6 this includes the base protocol specification, the operation of neighbor discovery protocols, and the techniques for auto-configuration of IPv6 addresses in Hosts.

6.1.1 Interpreting the IPv6 Basic Requirements Table

Interpreting the IPv6 Basic section of the Node Requirements Table requires understanding of the following configuration options and context definitions:

USGv6-V1 Host Requirements:
- [M] – **IPv6 Basic Requirements** – see section 6.1.
    - o [O:1] – **SLAAC** – require support of stateless address auto-configuration.
    - o [O:1] – **DHCP-Client** – require support of stateful (DHCP) address auto-configuration.
    - o [Y/N] – **PrivAddr** – require support of SLAAC privacy extensions.
    - o [Y/N] – **SEND** – require support of neighbor discovery security extensions.

USGv6-V1 Router Requirements:
- [M] – **IPv6 Basic Requirements** – see section 6.1.
    - o [Y/N] – **DHCP-Prefix** – require support of automated router prefix delegation.
    - o [Y/N] – **SEND** – require support of neighbor discovery security extensions.

The unconditional MUSTs (for both Hosts and Routers) in this category include support for the base *IPv6 Protocol Specification* [RFC2460], and the *Internet Control Message Protocol (ICMPv6)* [RFC4443]. Experience to date with these most basic protocols has led to the recent development of revisions and updates of these most basic specifications. In particular, we adopt the revised version of the ICMP specification, and the RFC that deprecates the use of type 0 Routing Headers [RFC5095] because of security concerns. We require Routers to recognize the router alert option [RFC2711], so as to enable Multicast Listener Discovery and other control protocols that require it. We indicate the intention (SHOULD+) to adopt Extended ICMP for Multi-Part Messages [RFC4884], in future versions of this profile.

Since IPv6 does not provide for packet fragmentation in Routers, both Hosts and Routers must conform to *Path MTU Discovery for IP Version 6* [RFC1981]. In addition, we require that both Hosts and Routers implement the full dynamic discovery procedures of RFC1981.

The *Neighbor Discovery* (ND) Protocol [RFC4861] is a reengineering of the IPv4 functions of Address Resolution, Router Discovery and ICMP Redirection and includes neighbor unreachability detection. It MUST be implemented by every IPv6 Node. Further, *IPv6 Node Requirements* [RFC4294] states that Hosts SHOULD implement ND Redirect functionality and Routers MUST implement it. This profile follows that requirement. The ND extensions to provide the ability to signal default router preference [RFC4191] provides an important capability that SHOULD+ be supported in Hosts and Routers. An expansion of the ND router advertisement flag encoding [RFC5175] has been defined and implementations SHOULD be prepared to process such encodings. It is expected that future versions of this profile will cite new protocols that require support of RFC5175 encodings.

While the potential threats to Neighbor Discovery are well documented [RFC3756], we must caution users to take care when considering the SEND configuration option. While *Secure Neighbor Discovery* [RFC3971] may be useful in some environments, there are concerns about its design and reliance on Cryptographically Generated Addresses (CGAs). It seems the IETF will launch an effort to define new, better solutions to this problem. While the profile allows users to select SEND, it would be premature to require or even recommend its support in all systems. Users that select the SEND configuration option should consult closely with potential vendors as to the availability of this capability.

The promise of plug-n-play auto configuration is a motivating factor for IPv6 adoption. Address Auto configuration is the method by which Hosts acquire global and local IPv6 addresses. Two models of IPv6 address auto configuration are provided in IPv6: *Stateless Address Auto configuration (SLAAC)* [RFC4862], and its stateful equivalent, *Dynamic Host Configuration Protocol for IPv6 (DHCPv6)* [RFC3315]. These two methods may be complementary, and are not necessarily mutually exclusive. This profile requires Hosts to support at least one method of address auto configuration. The configuration choices of SLAAC and DHCP-Client are thus [O:1].

Both Hosts and Routers are required to support the SLAAC procedures for creation of link local addresses and for detecting duplicate addresses on interfaces. Users can select the SLAAC configuration option to mandate the full support of SLAAC (for global addresses) on Hosts. It should be noted that when implemented, full SLAAC must have the capability to disable its use for global address assignment.

The privacy extensions for SLAAC [RFC4941] enable a node to vary its interface identifier over time in situations where eavesdropping and undesirable address-based tracking of Hosts is viewed as a significant threat. If the configuration option PrivAddr is selected, then these capabilities are a MUST, and are in general marked as SHOULD+ for Hosts that are required to be mobile nodes (MIP).

SLAAC is limited to the issues of address configuration. Typically Hosts require configuration of numerous other local environment variables (e.g., location of DNS/time/etc servers, domain name) in order to be truly plug-n-play. A subset of DHCP (below) has been defined [RFC3736] to augment SLAAC by providing such information. Hosts supporting SLAAC SHOULD+ support this capability.

The second option for auto configuration is the use of stateful (server-based) *Dynamic Host Configuration Protocol for IPv6 (DHCPv6)* [RFC3315]. If the Host configuration option DHCP-Client is selected, the client functions of RFC3315 MUST be supported. Like SLAAC, DHCP Hosts must support the ability to disable its use. The complexity of DHCP administration in dual-stack environments can be reduced if Hosts use consistent identifiers between their DHCPv4 and DHCPv6 requests. A DHCP extension [RFC4361] that enables this is indicated as SHOULD+ for this version of the profile.

While DHCP is not typically used to configure global IPv6 addresses for Routers, extensions to the protocol allow for Routers to receive address prefix delegations [RFC3633]. The configuration option DHCP-Prefix indicates the requirement to support this extension in routers. The notation c(M,S+) indicates the intent to include elevate this capability to an unconditional MUST in future versions of this profile.

6.2   Routing Protocols

The normative definition of technical requirements for this category is contained in the Routing Protocol Requirements section of the USGv6-V1 Node Requirements Table in Section 8. This section of the document provides informative discussion of the motivation for those requirements and additional information for clarification.

In the industry, routers are typically classified as being interior gateways (IGWs), or exterior gateways (EGWs). While this nomenclature is a bit dated, the real issue is whether the router supports intra-domain (enterprise) routing protocols, and/or inter-domain (global) routing protocols.   It is beyond the scope of this profile to provide a tutorial on the general differences and distinctions of these capabilities.   For the issues of routing in an IPv6 context, users of this profile are directed to the following RFCs for general descriptions of the issues surrounding routing IPv6 and IPv4-routing coexistence issues: [RFC4029] *Scenarios and Analysis for Introducing IPv6 into ISP Networks,* and [RFC2185] *Routing Aspects of IPv6 Transition.*

There are many aspects of transition mechanisms that are implemented by Routers and impact routing control plane functions. Users are directed to the section 6.4 Transition Mechanisms, for further discussion of these issues.

The USGv6-V1 Profile provides support for the two classes of routing protocols as indicated by the configuration options IGW and EGW. Typically an instance of a Router will support at least one class of routing protocol; often they will support both. The exceptions are simple customer premise equipment / stub routers and other simple forwarding devices that build forwarding tables in different ways.

It should be noted that there is a variety of choices for routing protocols, especially in the class of intra-domain.   This profile chooses a single protocol to serve as the common basis for interoperability among all IGW capable routers.   As with any other capability, this in no way prohibits the support of these other choices on a Router compliant to this profile, as long as the mandated protocol is also supported, and that support of any of the alternatives does not impede its correct operation.

6.2.1   Interpreting the Routing Protocol Requirements Table

Interpreting the Routing Protocol Requirements section of the Node Requirements Table requires understanding of the following configuration options and context definitions:

> **USGv6-V1 Router Requirements:**
> - [O] – **Routing Protocol Requirements** – see section 6.2.
>   - [Y/N] – **IGW** – require support of the intra-domain (interior) routing protocols.
>   - [Y/N] – **EGW** – require support for inter-domain (exterior) routing protocols.

Routers required to support IGW capabilities, MUST support *OSPF for IPv6* [RFC2740][5], as well as *Authentication/Confidentiality for OSPFv3* [RFC4552].

---

[5] A revised version of OSPF for IPv6 (RFC5340), obsoleting RFC2740, was released just before the publication of this profile. Given the recent date on the revised RFC, we are not mandating its support at this time, but fully expect to in future versions of this profile.

Routers required to support EGW capabilities MUST support *Border Gateway Protocol 4 (BGP4)* [RFC4271] and its enhancements for use in Internet applications [RFC1772], and enhancements requiring support of multiple protocols [RFC4760], in particular IPv6 [RFC2545].

6.2.2 Additional Routing Guidance

As noted in the section 1.3.6, this document limits its scope to the definition of IPv6 Requirements. There are many potential options and enhancements to protocols, not directly related to the support of IPv6, which might be desirable or required for a specific application; such issues are not addressed in these requirements. Also in some cases, IPv6 capabilities are enabled by extensions to existing IPv4 protocols; here, we only prescribe the IPv6-specific parts of such protocols. Users of this profile are required to specify the other requirements necessary to ensure completeness and quality of these other capabilities.

The standardized IPv6 routing protocols have many options and enhancements that may be required for specific uses. Examples might include support for BGP capabilities, such as: [RFC1997] *BGP Communities Attribute*; [RFC2918] *Route Refresh Capabilities for BGP-4*; [RFC3392] *Capabilities Advertisement with BGP-4*; and, [RFC4360] *BGP Extended Communities Attribute*. Similar extensions to OSPF for traffic engineering, resilience, etc are available, and must be specified by users of this profile as required.

6.3 Quality of Service

The normative definition of technical requirements for this category is contained in the Quality of Service Requirements section of the USGv6-V1 Node Requirements Table in Section 8. This section of the document provides informative discussion of the motivation for those requirements and additional information for clarification.

While many expect, or already believe, that IPv6 will deliver new Quality of Service (QoS) capabilities, the reality of the state of the technology is somewhat different. The development of new, scalable Quality of Service (QoS) mechanisms for IPv6 remains a work in progress. To date, the only mechanisms that have proven of general broad utility and viability are the support of Differentiated Services (DS) mechanisms in Routers.

It is the eventual goal of this profile to identify a small set of standardized DS behaviors that can form an interoperability base for the USG. However, at this time essential components for this base, such as Host DS signaling mechanisms and Router packet handling mechanisms (Per-Hop Behaviors or PHBs), do not seem to have reached a sufficient level of standardization and maturity. Hence, at this time, we only mark certain PHBs as SHOULD+, with the view that they will mandated in subsequent revisions of the profile.

While not technically a QoS mechanism, *Explicit Congestion Notification (ECN)* [RFC3168] provides a means for routers to signal congested paths to Hosts, and for Hosts to adjust traffic flows accordingly. Given its relationship to active queue management and throughput, we include its requirements in this section.

6.3.1 Interpreting the Quality of Service Requirements Table

Interpreting the Quality of Service section of the Node Requirements Table requires understanding of the following configuration options and context definitions:

USGv6-V1 Host Requirements:
- [O] – **Quality of Service Requirements** – see section 6.3.
  - [Y/N] – **DS** – require support of Differentiated Services capabilities.

USGv6-V1 Router Requirements:
- [M] – **Quality of Service Requirements** – see section 6.3.
  - [M] – **DS** – require support of Differentiated Services capabilities.

Selection of the DS configuration option in Hosts only requires that Hosts have the ability to encode the DS (Traffic Class) field of IPv6 packets according to the rules of [RFC2474] and [RFC3140]. All other issues of the interfaces and mechanisms necessary to control when these encodings are used are left for further refinement, although Host platforms SHOULD provide some means of doing so.

DS capabilities MUST be supported in Routers. This includes recognition of the same encoding rules as required for hosts: [RFC2474] and [RFC3140]. In addition, Routers SHOULD+ support a basic set of standardized PHBs, including those from the Assured Forwarding [RFC2597] and Expedited Forwarding [RFC3246] groups.

Hosts SHOULD support processing of the ECN bit in IPv6 packets, and Routers SHOULD+ support the procedures for setting the ECN bit.

6.3.2 Additional QoS Guidance

While the requirements above provide the building blocks for standardized / interoperable QoS mechanism, they are far from a full specification of a complete QoS system. Users of this profile who require a complete QoS system would need to additionally specify their required policy/configuration/API interfaces to QoS mechanisms, signaling and management protocols necessary for remote invocation/management and the security mechanisms necessary to guard against malicious and/or inadvertent use of these capabilities.

6.4 Transition Mechanisms

The normative definition of technical requirements for this category is contained in the Transition Mechanisms section of the USGv6-V1 Node Requirements Table in Section 8. This section of the document provides informative discussion of the motivation for those requirements and additional information for clarification.

It is expected that nodes and networks that support IPv4 will be deployed in Federal networks and the Internet for many years to come. The notion of a "Transition to IPv6", if taken literally, is a bit premature at this time. Instead what is needed at this stage is to develop carefully thought out plans for (a) how to safely adopt IPv6 in IPv4-dominant networks; (b) how to migrate application use to IPv6 in networks where it is available (moving towards IPv6-dominance); and, (c) how to ensure that IPv6-capable nodes retain the ability to interoperate with nodes which do not support IPv6 and across network infrastructures that do not provide native dual-stack forwarding services end to end.

The development of a well thought out coexistence and transition strategy is vital to successful adoption and use of IPv6 technologies. Much has been written about adoption and transition scenarios. We will not attempt to replicate that body of knowledge in this discussion. Users of this document are directed to the following general guidance documents on adoption and transition issues:
- **Enterprise Networks**:
  - o [RFC4057] *IPv6 Enterprise Network Scenarios.*
  - o [RFC4852] *IPv6 Enterprise Network Analysis - IP Layer 3 Focus.*
  - o [RFC3750] *Unmanaged Networks IPv6 Transition Scenarios.*
  - o [RFC3879] *Evaluation of IPv6 Transition Mechanisms for Unmanaged Networks.*
- **ISPs and Transit Network Infrastructure**:
  - o [RFC4029] *Scenarios and Analysis for Introducing IPv6 into ISP Networks.*
  - o [RFC2185] *Routing Aspects of IPv6 Transition.*
- **Interoperation with IPv4 Infrastructure**:
  - o [RFC4038] *Application Aspects of IPv6 Transition.*
  - o [RFC4213] *Basic Transition Mechanisms for IPv6 Hosts and Routers.*
- **USG Specific Guidance**
  - o [170] *Federal CIO Council IPv6 Transition Guidance.*

Users are cautioned to think carefully about the security implications of their adoption and transition plans. The adoption of a second protocol suite and the use of various transition mechanisms (e.g., tunneling) will complicate the job of adequately securing Federal IT systems. Users are encouraged to consult all appropriate sources in the development of adequate security plans, including *IPv6 Transition/Co-existence Security Considerations* [RFC4942].

The Host and Router profiles both contain a configuration option IPv4 to allow users to select whether support of IPv4 interoperability (i.e., "transition") mechanisms is required. Not choosing this option is equivalent to saying that the specified systems can be "IPv6-Only". Users are cautioned to think through carefully if systems can/should truly be IPv6-Only (including all configuration/management/monitoring interfaces), before deciding not to select the IPv4 option.

For systems that require interoperability with IPv4-only systems, the profile provides two basic mechanisms: dual-stack (native implementation of both protocols) and tunneling. For the scenario of interconnection "islands" of IPv6 over an IPv4 Multiprotocol Label Switching (MPLS) backbone, an additional mechanism is provided. This last scenario is common enough that we felt it warranted special attention.

The selection of dual-stack and simple tunneling mechanism purposefully tries to contain the potential complexity of a proliferation of IPv6/IPv4 interoperability mechanisms. Promoting a proliferation of other tunneling and translation schemes will only complicate the job of securing the overall network environment and will add undue risk to Federal information systems.

6.4.1 Interpreting the Transition Mechanisms Requirements Table

Interpreting the Transition Mechanism section of the Node Requirements Table requires understanding of the following configuration options and context definitions:

USGv6-V1 Host Requirements:
- [O] – **Transition Mechanism Requirements** – see section 6.4.
  - [Y/N] – **IPv4** – require support to enable interoperation with IPv4-only systems.

USGv6-V1 Router Requirements:
- [O] – **Transition Mechanism Requirements** – see section 6.4.
  - [Y/N] – **IPv4** – require support to enable interoperation with IPv4-only systems.
  - [Y/N] – **6PE** – require support of tunneling IPv6 over IPv4 MPLS services.

Hosts required to support IPv4 interoperability MUST support the dual-stack requirements of *Basic Transition Mechanisms for IPv6 Hosts and Routers* [RFC4213] and SHOULD support the use of configured tunnels. For reasons of configurability and security, we expect tunneling to mainly occur from Router-to-Router and thus leave the further specification of this capability on Hosts to users of this profile.

Routers MUST support both the dual stack and configured tunneling requirements of *Basic Transition Mechanisms for IPv6 Hosts and Routers* [RFC4213]. In addition, Routers MUST support *Using IPsec to Secure IPv6-in-IPv4 Tunnels* [RFC4891][6]. In addition, for IPv6-dominant scenarios Routers MUST support Generic *Packet Tunneling in IPv6* [RFC2473].

The Generic Routing Encapsulation [RFC2784] provides a generalized means of multiplexing multiple protocols over an underlying transmission mechanism and IPv6 encapsulation in GRE tunnels SHOULD+ be supported in Routers.

When the 6PE configuration option is selected, Routers MUST support *Connecting IPv6 Islands over IPv4 MPLS Using IPv6 Provider Edge Routers (6PE)* [RFC4798]. Note that this technique explicitly requires the use of BGP-4 to distribute IPv6 reachability information.

6.4.2 Additional Transition Mechanism Guidance

The 6PE transition mechanism relies on the existence of an IPv4-based MPLS infrastructure. Users of this transition mechanism must provide any additional requirements for capabilities (e.g., MPLS, label distribution protocols, etc) necessary to realize this approach.

---

[6] It should be noted that RFC4891 requires the support of transport mode Security Associations in routers. See the Node Requirements Table, under RFC4301 section 4.1 for the specific context and definition of the requirements.

6.5   Link Specific Capabilities

The normative definition of technical requirements for this category is contained in the Link Specific Requirements section of the USGv6-V1 Node Requirements Table in Section 8. This section of the document provides informative discussion of the motivation for those requirements and additional information for clarification.

What is specified here is how IPv6 interacts with and makes use of different link layer technologies; not the requirements of the technologies themselves. For link technologies that differ in ways not visible to IPv6 (e.g., wired and wireless Ethernet), no distinction is made in the profile.

In general we provide standardized mappings to a variety of link technologies commonly found in USG networks. Some of the older technologies maybe dropped from the profile over time as their utility diminishes. For bandwidth-constrained environments (e.g., low bit rate wireless) the profile provides various options for header and payload compression.

6.5.1   Interpreting the Link Specific Requirements Table

Interpreting the Link Specific section of the Node Requirements Table requires understanding of the following configuration options and context definitions:

USGv6-V1 Host Requirements:
- [M] – **Link Specific Technologies** – see section 6.5.
  - o   [O:1] – **Link** – require support of 1 or more link technologies.
  - o   [Y/N] – **ROHC** – require support of robust packet compression services.

USGv6-V1 Router Requirements:
- [M] – **Link Specific Technologies** – see section 6.5.
  - o   [O:1] – **Link** – require support of 1 or more link technologies.
  - o   [Y/N] – **ROHC** – require support of robust packet compression services.

Users of this profile must choose one or more [O:1] link technologies that MUST be supported for Routers and for Hosts. The Link configuration option / context variable should be interpreted in the following way. If Link=Ethernet is chosen, then the Link condition/context variable in the Node Requirements Table is considered TRUE (i.e. selected) for the *IPv6 over Ethernet* [RFC2464] requirement..

If the ROHC configuration option is selected, Nodes MUST support the *RObust Header Compression (ROHC) Framework* [RFC4995] and the supporting profiles for TCP [RFC4996], and RTP/UDP/ESP [RFC3095]. The IP-Only ROHC profile [RFC3843] SHOULD+ be supported. If ROHC is required on PPP links, the ROHC over PPP Profile [RFC3241] MUST be supported.

Older versions of compression of similar compression techniques (e.g., IP Header Compression [RFC2507]) are cited as OPTIONAL, strictly to highlight their existence should a profile user require interoperability with these techniques.

6.6 Addressing

The normative definition of technical requirements for this category is contained in the Addressing Requirements section of the USGv6-V1 Node Requirements Table in Section 8. This section of the document provides informative discussion of the motivation for those requirements and additional information for clarification.

A new, and vastly larger, address space is the most significant enhancement that IPv6 provides over IPv4. Beyond being much larger (128bit vs. 32bit), the IPv6 addressing architecture makes for the clear definition of multiple types of addresses (e.g., link-local, global, multicast, anycast) and multiple scopes of addresses (e.g., global, local, link).

Any adoption and deployment of IPv6 requires the development of an addressing plan. There are many significant issues associated with strategies for IPv6 address allocation and assignment. While many of these issues (e.g., provider independence, multi-homing, routing scalability, operational security) are critical to the eventual long term success of IPv6, they are beyond the scope of this specification. In particular, the process for acquiring and assigning IPv6 addresses within the Federal Government is outside the scope of this profile. Readers are directed to other USG guidance documents that cover some of these issues [168].

This profile's scope is limited to describing the requirements for Hosts and Routers to support specific IPv6 addressing capabilities. The only configuration option for addressing is related to the support of Cryptographically Generated Addresses (CGAs). Given the uncertain status of CGAs within the industry at this time, users are cautioned to consider carefully the maturity of CGA implementations before requiring their use.

6.6.1 Interpreting the Addressing Requirements Table

Interpreting the Addressing section of the Node Requirements Table requires understanding of the following configuration options and context definitions:

USGv6-V1 Host Requirements:
- [M] – **Addressing Requirements** – see section 6.6.
  - [Y/N] – **CGA** – require support of cryptographically generated addresses.

USGv6-V1 Router Requirements:
- [M] – **Addressing Requirements** – see section 6.6.
  - [Y/N] – **CGA** – require support of cryptographically generated addresses.

All Nodes MUST support the basic *IPv6 Addressing Architecture* [RFC4291] and its scoping mechanisms [RFC4007]. All Nodes MUST support the ability to manually configure global addresses, the ability to support multiple global addresses per interface and MUST follow the rules for *Default Address Selection* [RFC3484]. All Nodes SHOULD+ support the ability to configure these address selection policies. See section 6.9 for additional requirements on the format and use of Multicast IPv6 Addresses.

The use of the old Site-Local address type [RFC3879] is deprecated. The *Unique Local IPv6 Unicast Addresses* (ULA) [RFC4193] mechanism has been designed to fulfill a similar requirement. While *Private Addresses* are widely used in IPv4 networks, the generalized use and support of ULAs in IPv6 is not as mature nor is their architectural desirability as well understood. For these reasons, we make their support in this profile optional.

If the CGA or SEND configuration option is selected, Nodes MUST support Cryptographically Generated Addresses [RFC3972] and the enhancements [RFC4581] to support multiple hash algorithms [RFC4982].

See section 6.9 for additional requirements related to multicast addressing.

6.7 IP Security

The normative definition of technical requirements for this category is contained in the IP Security Requirements section of the USGv6-V1 Node Requirements Table in Section 8. This section of the document provides informative discussion of the motivation for those requirements and additional information for clarification.

The promise of delivering ubiquitous, scalable security at the IP level, and the potential to enable the realization of end-to-end security architectures is an often touted benefit of IPv6. In order to realize these goals, it is important that IP security (IPsec) capabilities be implemented fully and consistently across all systems. Providing a capable and ubiquitous network security capability will encourage the use of such capabilities in situations and applications that are not realized today.

To insure that interoperable, scalable security services are a standard capability of future Federal network, this profile requires support for IPsec and its key management protocols.

6.7.1 Interpreting the IP Security Requirements Table

Interpreting the IP Security section of the Node Requirements Table requires understanding of the following configuration options and context definitions:

USGv6-V1 Host Requirements:
- [M] – **IP Security Requirements** – see section 6.7.
  - o [M] – **IPsec-V3** – require support of the IP security architecture.
  - o [M] – **IKEv2** – require support for automated key management.
  - o [M] – **ESP** – require support for encapsulating security payloads in IP.

USGv6-V1 Router Requirements:
- [M] – **IP Security Requirements** – see section 6.7.
  - o [M] – **IPsec-V3** – require support of the IP security architecture.
  - o [M] – **IKEv2** – require support for automated key management.
  - o [M] – **ESP** – require support for encapsulating security payloads in IP.

There are no configuration options for IP Security. Consistent with the base *IPv6 Specification* [RFC2460] and the *IPv6 Node Requirements* [RFC4294], all Nodes compliant to this Profile MUST support IP Security capabilities.

IPsec is a suite of protocols that provides security to Internet communications at the network layer. The most common current use of IPsec is to provide a Virtual Private Network (VPN), either between two locations (gateway-to-gateway) or between a remote user and an enterprise network (host-to-gateway). IPsec can also provide end-to-end, or host-to-host, security. IPsec is also used by other Internet protocols (e.g. Mobile IPv6 (MIPv6)) to protect some or all of their traffic. When the payload of an IPsec packet is encrypted and data is in the form of cipher text, the use of traditional computer network defense mechanisms, such as network firewalls, filters, and packet inspection is complicated. While traditional tools can be adapted to work in the presence of IPsec, not all defenses possible with plaintext can be applied to IPsec encrypted traffic. For this reason, end-to-end (host-to-host) IPsec protection is less commonly employed, since it would require the enterprise Network Protection Devices (firewall, IDS, IPS) to allow the IPsec-encrypted traffic to enter the enterprise network without inspection by these devices. That would place the total responsibility for the enterprise's security on the host and/or the host's user, which is generally not viewed as a prudent approach in today's networks.

In order to use automated key management protocols such as the Internet Key Exchange (IKE) to negotiate and manage IPsec protections and secret keys between two peers, those peers must be able to definitively authenticate each other (i.e. verify each others' identities) in the course of the IKE negotiation. Pre-shared secret keys can be used for peer authentication within IKE; however, this method does not scale well. For large deployments, the initial provisioning and subsequent updating of the pre-shared secret keys are also problematic. Thus, the preferred method involves the use of Public Key Certificates or, for host-to-gateway IPsec, a combination of a certificate for the gateway and an Extensible Authentication Protocol (EAP)-based authentication method for the host. These methods require either a previous relationship between the peers, or the use of Public Key Certificates whose Certificate Authorities (CA) are mutually recognized. This is the reason that IPsec is most commonly used within a VPN, in which all peers receive their credentials from a single entity. Communication with formerly unknown peers is more problematic.

The protections provided by IPsec, and the protection that IKE provides to its own traffic, require the use of cryptographic algorithms, which include encryption algorithms (to provide confidentiality), MACs or Message Authentication Codes (to provide integrity protection), and PRFs or Pseudo-Random Functions (to generate secret keys and other values used within the IPsec protocols). Users of this profile should consult the scope and applicability statements of the most recent revision of FIPS 140 *Security Requirements for Cryptographic Modules* [154] to determine if additional procurement requirements apply to the specific intended use of cryptographic algorithms required by IPv6 IPsec and IKE implementations. While such additional requirements may apply to a given procurement, they are outside the scope of this profile and its definitions of compliance.

Currently, implementations are available for two versions of IPsec. The newer version, *IPsec-v3*, consisting of Architecture [RFC4301], Encapsulating Security Payload (ESP) [RFC4303] and Authentication Header (AH) [RFC4302], is preferred. *IPsec-v2*, consisting of previous versions of these specifications [RFC2401, RFC2406, and RFC2402] has been made obsolete by IPsec-v3, but is still the most commonly available version of IPsec. Some versions of IPsec-v2 have limited IPv6 capability, but this may not be sufficient for a complete IPv6 deployment. In the expectation that IPsec-v3 will be commonly available by the time the requirements of this profile is effective and that those implementations will have a more complete set of IPv6 features, this profile classifies support of IPsec-v3 as mandatory.

The IPsec ESP header provides confidentiality and/or integrity protection. The AH header provides integrity protection without confidentiality. Both ESP and AH provide data origin authentication, access control, and, optionally, replay protection. In transport mode, AH provides integrity protection to portions of the IP header, while ESP does not. In tunnel mode, both provide integrity protection to the inner IP header, but only AH protects portions of the outer header. However, AH presents its own security problems: it is a parallel execution path, with processing that is more complex than ESP. In many implementations, testing and implementation of AH is not as robust as that of ESP; some implementations do not include AH at all. When used in conjunction with IKE, ESP provides integrity-protection for two critical fields in the IP header: the source and destination addresses. As stated above, in tunnel mode ESP protects the complete inner IP header. For these reasons, this profile classifies AH as optional.

Null authentication (i.e. encryption only) is mandatory in IPsec-v2, but optional in IPsec-v3. However, if null authentication is used, the traffic must be integrity-protected through some other mechanism (e.g., a broader IPsec SA that also covers the segment with null authentication). This profile discourages the use of null authentication, except when used with combined-mode algorithms (see below). Furthermore, it is a basic requirement within the IPsec protocol that if null authentication is used, it must never be used together with null encryption.

Both AH and ESP with null encryption (ESP-NULL) provide integrity-protection without encryption. AH traffic can be identified through its protocol number; however, it should be noted that AH does not work in the presence of Network Address Translation (NAT). ESP-NULL presents a challenge for high-speed routers, firewalls, and other devices that want to definitively and efficiently distinguish between ESP-NULL traffic and ESP-encrypted traffic. One of the tasks of a newly-formed IETF Working Group, IPsec Maintenance and Extensions (ipsecme), is the development of "a standards-track mechanism that allows an intermediary device, such as a firewall or intrusion detection system, to easily and reliably determine whether an ESP packet is encrypted with the NULL cipher; and if it is, determine the location of the actual payload data inside the packet."[7] If that task produces a mature RFC, this profile will recommend its use. Until that time, agencies that require high-speed processing or inspection of integrity-protected packets using equipment that cannot be configured to efficiently handle the current ESP-NULL encapsulation, can modify this profile so as to require AH in their specifications,

All nodes MUST support both manual and automated management of Security Associations (SAs) and keys. The Internet Key Exchange (IKE) protocol has been redesigned and two versions are available. IKE version 2 (IKEv2) [RFC4306 and RFC4718] includes features, lacking in the original version of IKE, that are useful within IPv6. It is also the preferred key management protocol for IPsec-v3. Although IKEv2 implementations are currently relatively new, it is expected that IKEv2 implementations will be commonly available by the time this profile is effective. Thus IKEv2 MUST be supported in both Hosts and Routers.

Certificate format, contents and interpretation have been a source of interoperability problems within IPsec and IKE. Two recent RFCs, *Requirements for an IPsec Certificate Management Profile* [RFC4809] and *The IPsec PKI Profile of IKEv1/ISAKMP, IKEv2, and PKIX* [RFC4945] attempt to mitigate these problems. Their inclusion is strongly recommended (SHOULD+) in this version of the profile, but not mandated.

Cryptographic Algorithms within IPsec and IKE

IPsec security mechanisms are not tied to any specific cryptographic algorithms. Standard default algorithms are, however, specified in order to support interoperability. Complete IETF algorithm guidance is provided in [RFC4835] for AH and ESP, and [RFC4307] for IKEv2. A number of cipher suites are also defined in [RFC4308] and [RFC4869] for use within IPsec and IKE. These suites are intended to aid in interoperability and ease of configuration within the user GUI. However, different combinations of algorithms (other than the combinations defined in these suites) are both permissible and possible for both IPsec and IKE.

IKE relates to cryptographic algorithms in two distinct contexts. In the course of an IKE negotiation, IKE selects an encryption algorithm and an integrity protection algorithm to protect its own traffic (the IKE Security Association). IKE also negotiates the selection of an encryption algorithm and/or an integrity protection algorithm to protect future IPsec traffic between the negotiating peers (IKEv1's IPsec SA; IKEv2's child SA). In the IP Security part of the Node Requirements Table in section 8, the IKE SA algorithms are identified as "IKEv2" in the Condition/Context column; the ESP/AH algorithms are identified as "ESP," "AH," or "ESP or AH" in that column. The ESP/AH algorithms must be implemented in IPsec, and IKE must be capable of negotiating their use.

---

[7] The IETF ipsecme working group charter can be found at: http://www.ietf.org/html.charters/ipsecme-charter.html

As part of the peer authentication and key generation process, the IKE peers perform a Diffie-Hellman (DH) exchange. NIST SP 800-57, *Recommendation for Key Management – Part 1: General (Revised)* [156] contains guidance about how to choose the level of security needed for applications; it also contains requirements for Federal agencies when choosing key strengths based on the level of security chosen. Federal agencies may choose 80 bits of security (corresponding to IKE's DH group 2, a 1024-bit MODP group) until the end of 2010; after that, they can choose either 112 bits (i.e., a 2048-bit MODP group) or 128 bits. NIST SP 800-56A, *Recommendation for Pair-Wise Key Establishment Schemes Using Discrete Logarithm Cryptography (Revised)* [155] defines the required strengths for DH groups, including the size of the prime subgroup. DH group 24 (a 2048-bit MODP group defined in [RFC5114]) satisfies these requirements; DH group 14 (IKEv2's 2048-bit MODP group) does not. For that reason, this profile classifies DH group 24 as a MUST.

Although HMAC-SHA-1 [RFC2404] is still considered secure, the IETF is encouraging the standardization of HMAC-SHA-256 to ensure an orderly transition to a more secure MAC. *Using HMAC-SHA-256, HMAC-SHA-384, and HMAC-SHA-512 with IPsec* [RFC4868] defines the use of this family of algorithms as a MAC within IKE, ESP and AH; and as a PRF within IKE. Its inclusion in implementations of IPsec and IKEv2 is strongly recommended (SHOULD+). However, its use operationally is not generally necessary at this time.

AES-GCM [RFC4106] is a counter-based, combined-mode algorithm (provides both encryption and integrity protection) for ESP that is suitable for high-speed pipelining and parallel processing. AES-GMAC [RFC4543] is the variant of AES-GCM that provides authentication only. There are actually 2 AES-GMAC variants: the one that is used within AH is an integrity-protection algorithm, and the one that is used with ESP is a combined-mode algorithm, with null encryption, that provides integrity protection. These algorithms have a number of variants (both have multiple key sizes; AES-GCM has multiple ICV sizes) and are somewhat complex to use. Some of these complexities (cannot be used with manual keys) are imposed by the nature of the algorithm, but some are a result of the protocol definition (e.g., in IKE, key size must be specified for ESP, but for AH the transform ID includes the key size info, etc.). They are not yet widely implemented in IPsec implementations, and potential interoperability issues have not been addressed at IPsec interoperability events or by standardized testing organizations. Thus, at this time, they are designated as optional algorithms in this profile.

AES-GCM does not provide greater security than other AES modes (e.g. AES-CBC); however, it is more efficient than the other NIST-approved AES modes. At some point in the future, after operational experience has been gained, this profile will most likely upgrade it to a recommended algorithm (SHOULD+) and then to a mandatory one (MUST).

As computing capacity and speed increases, longer Diffie-Hellman (DH) values and larger digital signatures are required to provide adequate security. Elliptic curve algorithms can provide equivalent security, using significantly smaller values. Some applications find it cumbersome to provide sufficient security with MODP Diffie-Hellman or with RSA signatures, and future requirements for larger keys may exacerbate these problems. In the future, this profile will likely recommend the implementation and use of elliptic curve technology to reduce the burden on systems doing public cryptography. Currently, there are several hurdles to its use, including a lack of significant implementation, lack of interoperability testing, and vendor concern about numerous patent claims regarding the use of elliptic curve algorithms in digital certificates.

Since this profile does not currently mandate AES-GCM or elliptic curve cryptography, the IETF version of the Suite B cipher suite [RFC4869], which incorporates both, is optional. However, Suite B currently mandates the use of AES-CBC and HMAC-SHA-256 to protect IKEv2 traffic. Thus, implementations that incorporate the IETF's Suite B will still also incorporate these other algorithms as well. The AES-CBC encryption algorithm is included in most IKE and IPsec implementations, as is the HMAC-SHA-1 integrity protection algorithm. The HMAC-SHA-256 family of algorithms is designated SHOULD+ in this profile, and is expected to become widely implemented in the near future. As long as a node is not configured to only allow the use of Suite B, that node should be able to interoperate with implementations that conform to this profile.

Several of the algorithms (AES-CCM, AES-CTR, AES-GCM, and AES-GMAC) only retain their security properties if a given Initialization Vector (IV) is never used more than once with the same secret key. Therefore, these algorithms cannot be used with static (manually established) keys; they are secure only if used in conjunction with IKE or another secure key negotiation protocol. Furthermore, IKE negotiates different keys for both inbound and outbound traffic. If a key negotiation protocol is used that generates the same key for use in both directions, the peers must be sure to use different nonces (AES-CTR) or salts (AES-CCM, AES-GCM, AES-GMAC); otherwise, the algorithm's security is compromised.

The RFCs contain a contradiction related to the requirement level of the NULL encryption algorithm. In *Cryptographic Algorithms for ESP/AH* [RFC4835/section 3.1.1], null encryption is a MUST. However, in *Algorithms for IKEv2* [RFC4307/section 3.1.1], null encryption is a MAY, i.e., IKEv2 does not have to be able to negotiate null encryption for ESP. This profile makes null encryption a MUST.

In accordance with ESP-v3 [RFC4303/section 5] and *Cryptographic Algorithms for ESP/AH* [RFC4835/section 3.1.1], this profile designates null authentication as optional. As mentioned above, this profile discourages the use of null authentication, except when used with combined-mode algorithms (see below). Furthermore, it is a basic requirement within the IPsec protocol that if null authentication is used, it must never be used together with null encryption.

This draft also designates combined-mode algorithms (AES-CCM and AES-GCM) as optional. Since combined-mode algorithms provide both encryption and authentication, when they are used within IKE and IPsec the null authentication algorithm is selected as the integrity-protection algorithm. This use of null authentication is secure, since integrity-protection is provided by the combined-mode algorithm. In the future, if combined-mode algorithms are upgraded to SHOULD or MUST, null authentication will be similarly upgraded, but only for use with combined-mode algorithms.

6.8 Network Management

The normative definition of technical requirements for this category is contained in the Network Management Requirements section of the USGv6-V1 Node Requirements Table in section 8. This section of the document provides informative discussion of the motivation for those requirements and additional information for clarification.

In order to deploy networking infrastructures at scales larger than today's networks, both Hosts and Routers need scalable mechanisms to configure, monitor and manage their behavior. The Simple Network Management Protocol (SNMP) provides a means for automated remote management of IPv6 Nodes based upon Management Information Bases (MIBs) for IPv6 protocols.

To date, SNMP management has rarely been used in the industry for the management of Hosts. While the profile allows users to select SNMP for Hosts, users should investigate this requirement carefully, as the capability is often not implemented in Hosts. On the other, hand SNMP management of Routers is common in the industry, and support of these capabilities is mandatory for the Routers compliant to this profile.

6.8.1 Interpreting the Network Management Requirements Table

Interpreting the Network Management section of the Node Requirements Table requires understanding of the following configuration options and context definitions:

USGv6-V1 Host Requirements:
- [O] – **Network Management Requirements** – see section 6.8.
  - [Y/N] – **SNMP** – require support of network management services.

USGv6-V1 Router Requirements:
- [M] – **Network Management Requirements** – see section 6.8.
  - [M] – **SNMP** – require support of network management services.

As noted, SNMP is not typically used for management of Hosts. If the SNMP configuration option is selected for Hosts, then support for basic SNMP protocol [RFC3411] and capabilities [RFC3412, RFC3413, RFC3414] is required. For Hosts requiring SNMP, only support of the basic IP MIB is required [RFC4293]. Hosts supporting SNMP, SHOULD+ support of the TCP [RFC4022] and UDP [RFC4113] MIBs.

Routers MUST support SNMP management and the MIBs necessary to support the other mandatory capabilities of this profile. In particular, Routers MUST support the SNMP protocol [RFC3411] and related capabilities [RFC3412, RFC3413, RFC3414]. Routers MUST support MIBS for IP [RFC4293], Forwarding [RFC4292], IPsec [RFC4807], and DiffServ [RFC3289]. Additionally, if the appropriate configuration options are selected (IPv4 and MIP), additional MIBs for Tunnels [RFC4087] and MobileIP [RFC4295] MUST be supported also.

6.9 Multicast

The normative definition of technical requirements for this category is contained in the Multicast Requirements section of the USGv6-V1 Node Requirements Table in Section 8. This section of the document provides informative discussion of the motivation for those requirements and additional information for clarification.

IPv6 offers the promise of a more capable and complete support of multicast services than those typically found in IPv4 networks today. While the current state of IPv6 multicast technologies is not yet to the point that one could confidently include full support of generalized multicast as an unconditional MUST, the pieces are maturing, and we provide configuration options that allow users to require full support of Single Source Multicast (SSM) capabilities.

6.9.1 Interpreting the Multicast Requirements Table

Interpreting the Multicast section of the Node Requirements Table requires understanding of the following configuration options and context definitions:

USGv6-V1 Host Requirements:
- [M] – **Multicast Requirements** – see section 6.9.
  - o   [Y/N] – **SSM** – require full support of multicast communications.

USGv6-V1 Router Requirements:
- [M] – **Multicast Requirements** – see section 6.9.
  - o   [Y/N] – **SSM** – require full support of multicast communications.

Hosts and Routers MUST support the appropriate aspects of the Multicast Listener Discovery version 2 [RFC3810] capabilities. This basic capability is necessary to enable correct operation of link-multicast-based control protocols such as SLAAC, etc. This basic capability also provides an important foundation for more general multicast services should these be required later.

All uses of IPv6 multicast addresses must follow the basic requirements of the *IPv6 Addressing Architecture* [RFC4291] and refinements for Multicast addresses specified in *Allocation Guidelines for IPv6 Multicast Addresses* [RFC3307] and *Unicast-Prefix-based IPv6 Multicast Addresses* [RFC3306] .

The configuration option SSM allows the user to indicate the requirement for generalized Source Specific Multicast routing services. If selected, the SSM configuration option requires that Routers and Hosts support the appropriate parts of specifications for SSM packet processing [RFC4607] and the use of MLDv2 to manage SSM group membership [RFC4604].

Routers for which the SSM configuration option is specified, SHOULD+ support Protocol Independent Multicast – Sparse Mode (PIM-SM) [RFC4601] capabilities for multicast routing. Users requiring SSM routing capabilities should review the PIM-SM requirement and the security issues identified in [RFC4609] and augment this requirement if necessary. Routers supporting PIM-SM SHOULD+ also support capabilities for *Embedding the Rendezvous Point (RP) Address in an IPv6 Multicast Address* [RFC3956].

6.10 Mobility

The normative definition of technical requirements for this category is contained in the Mobility Requirements section of the USGv6-V1 Node Requirements Table in Section 8. This section of the document provides informative discussion of the motivation for those requirements and additional information for clarification.

IPv6 offers the promise of more efficient and more capable support of network layer mobility services than those realizable using IPv4. As more and more systems become nomadic, the needs for Mobile IP (MIP) capabilities will increase.

In general, MIP support is a selectable configuration option in this profile. While some form of mobility might well be a capability commonly required of future systems, it would seem premature at this point to make it more that a selectable option at this time. Users are informed that "mobility" is an issue that can be addressed at different layers and with different mechanisms. Care should be taken in identifying the type of mobility services actually required by a given use scenario. A second model of network layer mobility is provided by the NEMO configuration option. Network Mobility (NEMO) allows entire subnets of systems to be mobile behind the services of a NEMO-router.

6.10.1 Interpreting the Mobility Requirements Table

Interpreting the Mobility section of the Node Requirements Table requires understanding of the following configuration options and context definitions:

USGv6-V1 Host Requirements:
- [O] – **Mobility Requirements** – see section 6.10.
  - o [Y/N] – **MIP** – require support of mobile IP mobile node capabilities.

USGv6-V1 Router Requirements:
- [O] – **Mobility Requirements** – see section 6.10.
  - o [Y/N] – **MIP** – require support of mobile IP home agent capabilities.
  - o [Y/N] – **NEMO** – require support of mobile network capabilities.

All nodes must maintain the capability to forward (Routers) and process (Hosts) packets from a mobile node (MN). The unconditional requirements for these capabilities listed in the profile, are actually just reinforcements of basic IPv6 protocol requirements.

Selecting the configuration option MIP for Hosts requires support for MIPv6 [RFC3775], including the capability to perform as a Mobile Node (MN) and as a Correspondent Node (CN) with route optimization capabilities. Such Hosts MUST support *Mobile IPv6 Operation with IKEv2 and the Revised IPsec Architecture* [RFC4877] to secure MIP signaling.

Selecting the MIP configuration option for Routers requires support for MIPv6 [RFC3775], including the capability to perform as a MIP Home Agent (MIP HA). Such Routers MUST also support *Mobile IPv6 Operation with IKEv2 and the Revised IPsec Architecture* [RFC4877] to secure MIP signaling.

Selecting the NEMO configuration options for Routers requires support for the Network Mobility (NEMO) Basic Support Protocol [RFC3963].

6.11 Application Requirements

The normative definition of technical requirements for this category is contained in the Application Requirements section of the USGv6-V1 Node Requirements Table in Section 8. This section of the document provides informative discussion of the motivation for those requirements and additional information for clarification.

In general, the scope of this profile is limited to specifying the technologies necessary to provide a basic IPv6 networking capability in Hosts and Routers. It seems premature and inadvisable to attempt to broadly mandate capabilities and constraints for the vast number and variety of applications that comprise modern networked IT environments. Instead, we focus on a few specific control plane application protocols that are necessary to support basic IPv6 networking capabilities, provide some conditional recommendations about the interfaces necessary to make IPv6 capabilities available to applications and users, and provide some general guidance that agencies can use to further develop their own additional requirements and specifications of further application issues.

In general, we classify applications and application protocols as those that operate above the Transport Layer (i.e., above TCP/UDP/RTP, etc). This includes both traditional user-oriented applications (e.g., SMTP/email, HTTP/web) and those control protocols (e.g., SNMP, IKE, BGP, DNS, DHCP) necessary to support basic IPv6 networking capabilities. Of course this scope also includes a vast array of other standard, custom, proprietary, and/or new applications.

The technical requirements of control plane protocols such as SNMP, IKE, BGP and DHCP have been specified in other sections of this profile. The Application Requirements section of the USGv6-V1 Node Requirements Table specifies the protocol requirements for one additional control protocol necessary for the provision of Domain Name System (DNS) services within the network. In addition, this section provides conditional requirements on the capabilities of some classes of Application Programming Interfaces (APIs), User Interfaces (UIs) and uses of Resource Identifiers. Finally this section provides general guidance to agencies to use in the further definition of requirements for specific applications.

6.11.1 Interpreting the Application Requirements Table

Interpreting the Application section of the Node Requirements Table requires understanding of the following configuration options and context definitions:

USGv6-V1 Host Requirements:

- [O] – **Application Requirements** – see section 6.11.
    - [Y/N] – **DNS-Client** – require support of DNS client/resolver functions.
    - [Y/N] – **Sock** – require support of Socket application program interfaces.
    - [Y/N] – **URI** – require support of IPv6 uniform resource identifiers.
    - [Y/N] – **DNS-Server** – require support of a DNS server application.
    - [Y/N] – **DHCP-Server** – require support of a DHCP server application.

USGv6-V1 Router Requirements:

- [O] – **Application Requirements** – see section 6.11.
    - [Y/N] – **DNS-Client** – require support of DNS client/resolver functions.
    - [Y/N] – **URI** – require support of IPv6 uniform resource identifiers.
    - [Y/N] – **DNS-Server** – require support of a DNS server application.
    - [Y/N] – **DHCP-Server** – require support of a DHCP server application.

If the configuration option URI is selected, Nodes MUST comply with Uniform Resource Identifier: Generic Syntax [RFC3986] – which permits an IPv6 address to appear anywhere an IPv4 address can. This requirement applies to URI uses in User Interfaces, APIs, protocols, configuration scripts, etc.

Detailed specifications of language bindings and API sets are beyond the scope of this profile. While we include the SOCK configuration option, which covers the C language API bindings described in several Informational RFCs, this by itself will typically not be sufficient for application programming purposes; users needing such capabilities should consider augmenting/replacing this option with more complete specifications such as POSIX[8] [175] if appropriate

In the case when the configuration option SOCK is selected, Hosts MUST provide the Basic [RFC3493] and SHOULD provide the Advanced [RFC3542] Socket APIs for IPv6. In addition, such Hosts that require support of Mobility (MIP) or Source Specific Multicast (SSM) capabilities MUST support the corresponding Socket API extensions [RFC3542, RFC4584, RFC3678].

If the configuration option DNS-Client is selected, Nodes MUST support the basic DNS protocol extensions for incorporating IPv6 into DNS resource records [RFC3596] and MUST provide support DNS message extension mechanism [RFC2671] and message size requirements [RFC3226]. These specifications address the basic format of IPv6 related DNS resource records and their transmission in DNS messages. There are many other practical issues related to deploying IPv6 DNS capabilities that should be considered, including:

- Users are advised that there are numerous issues regarding the operational configuration and use of the DNS in dual stack and transition scenarios. See the section on Transition Mechanism Requirements for DNS operational requirements posed by *Basic Transition Mechanisms for IPv6 Hosts and Routers* [RFC4213] and *Operational Considerations and Issues with IPv6 DNS* [RFC4472].

- Nodes that are required to support an IPv6 DNS Server capability (DNS-Server) must be specifically identified. Users of this profile must specify any additional capabilities required of DNS-Servers beyond the basic IPv6 capabilities specified in [RFC3596].

6.11.2 Additional Application Guidance

The detailed specification of application specific IPv6 requirements is beyond the scope of this version of the profile. Beyond the application environment requirements explained above, users of this profile must provide any additional technical requirements to be met by specific applications. The following general guidance may be useful in the formulation of such additional requirements.

There is no single definition of what it means to be an "IPv6-capable application". For dual-stack applications (that also operate over IPv4), we can provide the following guidance as to how one might define its corresponding IPv6 requirements:

1. Dual-stack applications should be able to operate in "IPv6 only", and mixed IPv6/IPv4 environments, with no less functionality than is currently available in their use in pure IPv4 environments. In more detail, this implies:

---

[8] POSIX® is a registered trademark of the Institute of Electrical and Electronic Engineers, Inc.

a. The application works normally (including configuration, monitoring and management) on nodes with no IPv4 capabilities (e.g., either not implemented or administratively disabled).

b. The application works normally in dual stack environments and selects which underlying protocol stack (IPv4 or IPv6) to use on a per-instance of communication basis. Such stack selection should follow the rules of basic transition mechanisms as modified by locally configured policies.

c. The application works normally on IPv4-only nodes (e.g., IPv6 either not implemented or administratively disabled).

The practical implications of the above guidance will vary with applications and specific implementation environments (e.g., operating systems, execution environments/platforms, etc). Some applications will run over IPv6 with no code changes (e.g., if they simply open a TCP connection and run simple protocols). Other applications will need to be modified to remove any IPv4 dependencies and to add support for IPv6. The following lists some of the common issues that will require code modifications to support IPv6 at the application level.

- If the application has a user interface (UI) that allows the user to enter an IP address (e.g., as part of a specifying a configuration), the UI must also support entry of IPv6 addresses.

- If the application displays IP addresses, then IPv6 addresses must be displayed appropriately.

- If the application parses text that may contain an IP address (e.g., as part of URI processing), such code must also support IPv6 addresses.

- If the application stores any information in files (e.g., in a cache), and that information can include IP addresses, it must be possible to store IPv6 addresses as well.

- If the application runs a private protocol with a peer, and the message flows include IP-address specific information (e.g., a specific IP address), the protocol needs to be updated to support the transport of IPv6 information as well.

- If the application stores IP addresses in binary format, then it should make use of protocol agnostic structures (e.g., sockaddrs), rather than, say 4-byte integers, so that it will automatically be able to handle IPv6's longer addresses.

Users of this profile must supply any additional requirements (beyond those documented in the Node Requirements Table) that must be met by specific applications.

6.12 Network Protection Device Requirements

The normative definition of technical requirements for this category is contained in the Network Protection Device Requirements section of the USGv6-V1 Node Requirements Table in Section 8. Having said that, there is a complete lack of public specifications for the capabilities and required behaviors of Network Protection Devices (NPDs). To fill that void, we outline the minimal required capabilities of such devices in this section.

Should other viable public specifications of Firewall and/or IDS capabilities become available over time, this profile would evolve to adopt them by reference. But, given the importance of IPv6 Network Protection Devices to the safety and security of Federal IT systems that adopt IPv6, we provide our own specification of their minimum mandatory capabilities at this time.

6.12.1 Interpreting the Network Protection Device Requirements Table

Interpreting the Network Protection Device section of the Node Requirements Table requires understanding of the following configuration options and context definitions:

USGv6-V1 NPD Requirements:
- [M] – **Network Protection Device Requirements** – see section 6.12.
    - o [O:1] – **FW** – require support of basic firewall capabilities.
    - o [O:1] – **APFW** – require support of application firewall capabilities.
    - o [O:1] – **IDS** – require support of intrusion detection capabilities.
    - o [O:1] – **IPS** – require support of intrusion protection capabilities.

Given the lack of public consensus standards in this area, this section serves as the primary source of NPD requirements. Thus this section provides both the definition of the requirements cited in the Node Requirements Table and background for its interpretation.

Network protection devices (firewalls, intrusion detection systems (IDS), intrusion prevention systems (IPS) and the like) are currently essential for securing external network connections in the IPv4 world. This situation will no doubt continue with IPv6; while new technologies (enabled in part by IPv6 and IPsec) hold out the promise of true end-to-end security, network perimeter security will continue to be play a needed role. In the near term, this need is especially pressing; indeed, unlike with the original introduction of IPv4, no significant "grace period" for the development of strong IPv6 network protection technology can be expected, as hackers are already developing attack suites for IPv6 networks.

Given this situation, it is essential that IPv6 network protection devices which are just as capable as their IPv4 counterparts be immediately available coincident with the introduction of IPv6 into government networks. Ensuring this capability exists is the goal of these requirements.

The requirements listed here concentrate on the IPv6-specific features required for network protection devices. Any other features an agency requires for its network devices (e.g., support for a particular administrative model or a special authentication method) are to be addressed through the agency's usual specification and validation methods.

In particular, IPv4-only features are not addressed here. While it is to be expected that IPv4 traffic will continue for the foreseeable future, and hence IPv4 network protection devices will be required, an agency can choose to use separate network protection devices for IPv4 and IPv6 traffic. Hence, even for devices which offer both IPv4 and IPv6 network protection features, this profile only addresses their IPv6 functionality.

In general, these requirements seek merely to establish the minimal threshold of functionality required for IPv6 network protection devices. For firewalls, this means basic port-blocking and (for application firewalls) application data filtering, while for intrusion detection and prevention systems, this means the ability to detect (and, in the case of IPSs, to prevent or disrupt) known attack patterns, including IPv6 version of known IPv4 attacks. In both cases, network protection devices will typically offer other more sophisticated features, such as statistical anomaly detection, but given the minimal nature of these requirements, they will not be addressed here.

6.12.2 Source of requirements

The sort of functionality provided by network protection devices is not well-covered by protocol or interoperability specifications such as Internet RFCs. Hence, we cannot create the same sort of profiles as for Host systems or Routers, where we can specify desired functionality by listing relevant RFCs and options. Instead, we must list all requirements explicitly.

There are, however, two lists of firewall requirements we have used as reference sources in composing this list: the *Internet Protocol Version Six Information Assurance Test Plan* [162] from the DoD, and the *ICSA Labs Modular Firewall Certification Criteria* [165] version 4.1. Our firewall requirements in the main follow these documents, though as mentioned above, we concentrate solely on that functionality required for IPv6. Additional sources used to derive the functional requirements of this profile include IPv6 firewall design and discussion documents such as [163] and [164].

By contrast, there are no comparable lists of functionality requirements for intrusion detection and prevention systems. NIST Special Publication 800-94, *Guide to Intrusion Detection and Prevention Systems* [158], and NIST IR 7007, *An Overview of Issues in Testing Intrusion Detection Systems* [159] do however discuss the sorts of functionality provided by these systems and the challenges involved in testing them.

6.12.3 Common requirements for network protection devices

6.12.3.1 Basic host or router IPv6 connectivity requirements

While network protection devices are technically, in terms of their connection characteristics, either hosts or routers, they are not typically expected to provide the same level of functionality, unless they are part of some combined device (such as a firewall-router).

More commonly, network protection devices only implement basic protocol capabilities to the extent necessary to perform their security functions while not interfering with the interoperability of desirable traffic passing through them. This typically includes basic protocol parsing, address recognition, link encapsulation, etc. Often many other basic protocol functions (e.g., error reporting, auto configuration) are implemented in non-standard ways on such devices or omitted.

Given the variance of capability and behavior of these basic IPv6 connectivity requirements in NPDs, we do not attempt to specify them in detail here. Instead we focus on the specification of their network security capabilities. Certainly for combined devices, users of this profile can specify that a protection device comply with the requirements of both a Router and a firewall (for example).

6.12.3.2 Dual stack

While it is expected that most network protection devices will provide protection functionality for both IPv4 and IPv6 traffic, only IPv6 protection functionality is addressed here. Other functionality (such as administrative interfaces) MAY be available over only one network stack (generally IPv4).

6.12.3.3 Administrative functionality

A network protection device must offer sufficient administrative controls to allow effective use of the facilities it offers. This includes controls over the configuration of its protective functionality, its logging and alert facilities, and access to the administrative facilities themselves. Such administrative functionality MUST be available either directly on the device console or equivalent, or through remote communications using openly-defined means.

6.12.3.4 Authentication and authorization

All administrative access to a network protection device MUST be controlled through appropriate authentication mechanisms, and restricted to appropriately authorized users. In the case of network protection devices which do not separate administrative roles, authentication as an administrator can be viewed as sufficient authorization.

6.12.3.5 Security of control and communications

All administrative controls MUST be secure from non-authorized access, and all administrative communications with a network protection device must be secure from outside observation. This can be done through local console-type access; through FIPS-approved encrypted network communication; or through network communications which are secured through other means from outside access (such as VLAN separation or firewall blocking).

6.12.3.6 Persistence

All device settings MUST persist through loss and restoration of electrical power.

6.12.3.7 Logging and alerts

Network protection devices MUST provide sufficient administrative capability to allow inspection of all administratively-controlled settings and give assurance of their proper functioning. Such capability MUST be controllable by, and accessible to, properly authorized administrators.

Intrusion detection systems have additional logging requirements, as described below.

6.12.3.8 Fragmented packet handling

Network protection devices MUST be able to handle fragmented packets, whether by provisionally reassembling and applying appropriate controls based on the reassembled packet, or (in the case of firewalls) by blocking fragments that cannot otherwise be handled.

6.12.3.9 Tunneled traffic handling

Network protection devices MUST be able to handle all v4/v6 tunneling schemes, no matter how embedded, either by analyzing and applying the appropriate controls based on the encapsulated packet header, or (in the case of firewalls) by simply blocking all unanalyzed tunneled packets.

6.12.4 Firewall requirements

6.12.4.1 Common (port-blocking) requirements

6.12.4.1.1 Port/protocol/address blocking

Firewalls MUST allow selective blocking/admission of traffic by protocol, and, for IPv6 packets, by source and/or destination subnet and/or address, by extension header type and, for higher-level protocols, by the appropriate per-protocol subfields - ports for UDP and TCP, and type and code for ICMP. Such blocking/admission MUST be equally effective for both normal and IPsec traffic; the latter to the extent such fields are visible in the packet.

Port blocking/admission functionality MUST be sufficiently rich to allow discrete controls in both directions down to the individual port level, for any desired ports. While it is desirable to be able to block/admit any possible combination of ports, at a minimum the port-blocking functionality MUST have sufficient capacity to selectively include or exclude all commonly used services.

Address blocking functionality MUST be sufficiently rich to allow blocking of all traffic with source or destination addresses which ought not to be present in traffic sent between external and internal networks, such as local addresses (including loopback, link local, site local, and RFC4193-style unique local addresses), or source multicast addresses.

Firewalls MUST allow blocking of all traffic which has not been explicitly authorized.

6.12.4.1.2 Asymmetrical blocking

Firewalls MUST, either through software or hardware configuration, distinguish between external and internal connected networks, and allow imposing asymmetrical controls on traffic between these networks. In particular, for connection-oriented protocols such as TCP, firewalls MUST have the ability to allow bidirectional traffic flow over connections initiated from hosts on the internal network to hosts on the external network, while blocking connection initiation from the external network.

For request/response protocols without explicit connection setup (e.g., ICMP echo request and reply), firewalls SHOULD be able to selectively block unsolicited (vs. solicited) replies coming from the external network.

6.12.4.1.3 IPsec traffic handling

Firewalls MUST either be capable of terminating IPsec connections (security gateways), or be capable of selectively blocking IPsec traffic.

6.12.4.1.4 Performance under load, fail-safe

When firewalls suffer operational degradation or failure due to high network loads or other factors, they MUST fail in such a manner as not to allow unauthorized access.

6.12.4.2 Application firewall requirements

6.12.4.2.1 No violation of trust barriers

Application firewall mediation of data transversal (session, file, etc.) through the firewall MUST NOT violate trust barriers, either by improperly rewriting incoming untrusted data to appear trusted, or by improperly exposing information (such as internal network structures) to external untrusted networks.

6.12.4.2.2 Session traffic authorization

Application firewalls MUST have means of controlled authorization for the establishment of sessions initiated from the external network to internal hosts.

6.12.4.2.3 Email, file filtering

Application firewalls MUST have configurable means for examining files (such as email attachments) that are transferred from the external network to internal hosts for the presence of undesired elements, and, when such elements are found, selectively blocking or stripping them. The means of detection used varies with the firewall, ranging from pattern (signature)-matching or other heuristics for virus detection, to the simple blocking of, for example, all executable file content. In any case, the means MUST be sufficient to block typical threat traffic.

6.12.5 Intrusion detection and prevention system requirements

6.12.5.1 Common (detection) requirements

6.12.5.1.1 Known attack detection

Intrusion detection systems MUST provide a configurable capability to detect suspicious traffic based on known attack patterns, including those embedded in HTTP and SMTP traffic.

6.12.5.1.2 Malformed packet detection

Intrusion detection systems MUST detect malformed packet types, such as non-standard or unassigned protocols, reserved header bits being set, undefined ICMP codes, improper (e.g., local or undefined) packet addresses, bad fragment offsets and impossible TTL values.

6.12.5.1.3 Port-scanning detection

Intrusion detection systems MUST detect typical port scanning (multiple ports of a single host) and host scanning (single port across multiple hosts) techniques, including "stealth" scans. (Note that while "blind" host scanning across a subnet is not considered feasible for IPv6, other techniques such as scanning based on DNS data are still a concern.)

6.12.5.1.4 Tunneled traffic detection

Intrusion detection systems MUST be able to detect threat patterns even for tunneled traffic, when packet data contents may be embedded with multiple IP (v6/v4) headers. For tunneling methods for which content examination is not supported, it is sufficient merely to flag all such tunneled packets.

6.12.5.1.5 Logging and alerts

Intrusion detection systems MUST provide means to log all suspicious traffic and send notification to the appropriate administrators.

6.12.5.1.6 Performance under load, fail-safe

When intrusion detection systems suffer operational degradation or failure due to high network loads or other factors, they MUST provide notification of such failure. In cases of overload, intrusion detection systems SHOULD prioritize their processing to preferentially examine the highest-risk traffic.

6.12.5.2 Intrusion prevention requirements

6.12.5.2.1 Intrusion prevention

Intrusion prevention devices MUST implement the intrusion detection capabilities listed in the previous section. In addition, intrusion prevention devices MUST provide means to stop or attenuate detected attacks, either (when inline) directly or through manipulation of other network devices (e.g., updating a router ACL or firewall rule set). Such prevention means include dropping or rejecting suspect packets, throttling bandwidth usage from suspect sources, or rewriting or removing malicious content.

7.   Compliance

This section describes procedural and documentation requirements for products claiming compliance with this profile. The foundation for all claims of compliance shall be based upon a product conformance and interoperability testing program comprised of open consensus test suites, formally accredited testing laboratories, and approved accreditation bodies.

Primarily, the means of expression of compliance for a specific product will be through a *Supplier's Declaration of Conformity* (SDOC), as specified in ISO/IEC 17050[174]. The SDOC is backed by a chain of traceability of results through laboratories accredited under ISO/IEC 17025 *General Requirements for Testing Laboratories* [172], and specific test methods as described in NIST SP-500-273 *IPv6 Test Methods: General Description and Validation* [160]. To be recognized in this program, test laboratories must be accredited by an accreditation body compliant to ISO/IEC 17011 *Conformity assessment – General requirements for accreditation bodies accrediting conformity assessment bodies* [171], and subject to peer review as a signatory to the International Laboratory Accreditation Conference, ILAC.

The issue of compliance life cycles, conditions for compliance, requirements for the SDOC and the details of the testing program are discussed in successive subsections below .

7.1   Compliance Life Cycles

The profile embodied in this document is a strategic planning tool for procurement officials, IPv6 product suppliers, testing laboratories, test product suppliers and laboratory accreditation bodies. One implication of developing a forward looking profile is that it is unreasonable to expect the product and testing industry to be able to respond immediately to new mandatory requirements as soon as they are published. Likewise, users and procurement officials need adequate time to plan for the acquisition and deployment of new capabilities. As a general principle, we recommend that users and the product industry be given 24 months between the publication of a significant new mandatory requirement and citations of those requirements in procurement actions. New incremental requirements should be given 12 months before citation in procurement actions. The Effective Date for each mandatory requirement is indicated in the Node Requirements Table. This represents the earliest date that acquisition authorities should require demonstrated compliance to each distinct profile mandatory requirement.

In the future, we plan to issue a new version of this profile at most once per year. We consider the marking of a requirement as SHOULD+ (S+) as the indication of the intent to add a new mandatory requirement in a subsequent version of the profile. As a general principle, in future revisions of the profile, no requirement will be made mandatory, that was not indicated as SHOULD+ in the previous version. Thus significant new requirements will be given at least 36 months between their effective dates and the date of the publication of a version of the profile that had the same requirement flagged as SHOULD+[9].

In this first version of the profile, the effective date of all mandatory requirements in the Node Requirements Table is set to July of 2010 (24 months after the publication of USGv6V1). The next

---

[9] This does not preclude holding a feature at SHOULD+ over several iterations of the profile, while monitoring the maturation of that technology.

planned revision of this profile will be published no sooner than 12 months after the publication of version 1, and will proceed on a yearly cycle after that.

As products and profiles evolve, the issues of compliance life cycle management can grow complex. In general, as new versions of the profile emerge, we recommend that users cite the most recent version of this profile while paying close attention to the effective dates of its requirements. The details of how profile evolution and product evolution affect the validity of test results shall be addressed in the management plan for the USGv6 test program, but in general it is the objective of this test program to avoid gratuitous retesting of products where product enhancements or profile changes should not materially affect previous test results.

7.2 Conditions for Compliance

The minimal mandatory set of IPv6 capabilities for each device category (Host, Router and Network Protection Device) is defined by the corresponding unconditional MUSTs in the Node Requirements Table. This set of requirements defines the minimal capabilities of a Host, Router or NPD that claims to be "USGv6-V1-Capable".

Compliance to this profile is defined in terms of all of the capabilities claimed or required. That is, compliance is required, tested and reported to the set of unconditional MUST requirements, plus those MUSTs that are conditional on options required for a particular procurement request or claimed for a specific product. Hence, being "USGv6-V1-Compliant" is only meaningful with respect to a specific set of conditions and configuration options. The conditions and configuration options are defined in the Host, Router and NPD profile templates in sections 3, 4, and 5 (and further explained in section 6) and employed to define mandatory requirements in the Node Requirements Table of Section 8.

The details of each aspect of this testing program are provided in the sections that follow.

7.3 Laboratory Accreditation

Internationally recognized systems of testing include traceability of tests to a designated set of standard reference materials and accountability of testing through to the International Laboratory Accreditation Cooperation (ILAC). Test methods and the accreditors are usually chosen by the program sponsor, which is NIST for this program. In this section and the next the relationships between Test Laboratories, Accreditation Bodies, Test Suites and Test methods are described.

7.3.1 Testing Laboratories

Testing laboratories are accredited based on their compliance with ISO/IEC 17025 *General Requirements for Testing Laboratories*, together with NIST SP 500-273 *IPv6 Test Methods: General Description and Validation*. Three classes of testing laboratory are identified[10]:
- First party laboratories - are owned or controlled by an IPv6 product supplier, and may be used to produce conformance testing results.
- Second party laboratories - are owned or controlled by a USG acquisition authority.
- Third party laboratories - are independent (typically fee-for-service) bodies.

---

[10] Information pertaining to Accreditors and Test Laboratories will be kept current at the website http://www.antd.nist.gov/usgv6/.

Conformance testing results for Hosts and Routers can originate from each class of laboratory. Interoperability testing results for Hosts and Routers may only originate in a second or third party testing laboratory. Testing of Network protection devices requires a somewhat different approach to the program. Here, the industry norms call for recognition of the results of testing only from second or third party accredited laboratories. In all cases, for any type of testing result to be recognized by this program, the tests must be performed by an accredited laboratory.

7.3.2 Accreditation Bodies

Accreditation bodies are recognized in this program by their adherence to ISO/IEC 17011 *Conformity Assessment – General requirements for accreditation bodies accrediting conformity assessment bodies [171]*, and their status as signatories to the International Laboratory Accreditation Cooperation (ILAC).

Accreditation bodies of interest to this program will establish methods of accreditation for laboratories testing Information Technology systems in accordance with the procedures and processes outlined in this document and NIST SP-500-273 *IPv6 Test Methods: General Description and Validation* [160].

7.4 Test Methods

The chain of traceability for compliance test results is rooted in abstract test specifications. These test suites will be validated against public specifications (mainly IETF RFCs) and serve as the standard reference material for this test program. The genesis of these tests specifications, their evolution, and use in accredited testing laboratories are given in successive subsections, below.

7.4.1 Abstract Test Suites for Hosts and Routers

The IPv6 Forum has created test specifications for conformance and interoperability of Hosts and Routers to a series of subsets of IPv6 capabilities [151]. The IPv6 Forum's IPv6Ready logo program has made significant progress in the development of abstract test suites and test methods that embody significant vendor consensus and international coordination. Given the concerns about proliferation of testing requirements and the need for international harmonization expressed at the first NIST workshop on IPv6 Testing, it is appropriate to adopt the IPv6 Forum's testing materials, where possible and relevant, to serve as the basis for development of this test program.

Through the execution of Memoranda of Understanding (MOU) between NIST and the developers of various IPv6 Forum test suites, the IPv6Ready tests will be adopted as a starting point for the USG IPv6 test program. While there is much that will be leveraged from the IPv6 Forum's effort, it is important to note that the existing IPv6Ready tests and test results are not based upon this USG profile. Considerable development and refinement of these tests will be necessary to adapt them to test this specific profile and to complete suites for functionality currently not covered by the IPv6Ready logo program. In addition, the MOUs also document the goal of maintaining harmonization between the IPv6 Forum and USG tests where ever possible.

The procedures for the enhancement, vetting, publication and validation of test suites and methods for this program will be coordinated with the IPv6 Forum and further documented in NIST SP-500-273.

7.4.2 Network Protection Device Test Methods

At the time of publication of this profile there are no publicly available test suites for Network Protection Devices, and no freely available testing devices, or procedures. NIST will undertake to work with the product industry, other Government agencies and the commercial testing industry to define a suitable test program for these devices. Given the nature of testing of security devices, the level of specification and means of validation and accreditation of such test suites may differ from than those of common Routers and Hosts. As the NPD test program is developed, NIST will evaluate if additional guidance documents are needed in this area.

7.4.3 Suppliers Declaration of Conformity

The conditions for device compliance to this profile are stated in section 7.2 above. IPv6 device suppliers must use the Supplier's Declaration of Conformity, (SDOC), ISO/IEC 17050 Parts 1 and 2 to document claims of support of: (i) protocols/functions listed in the Node Requirements Table, and (ii) specific functions called out from the body of each specification and listed as MUST, SHOULD+, SHOULD or MAY. Note that it is not necessary to claim support of functions classified as SHOULD+, SHOULD or MAY. But such functions MUST be tested if they are claimed, and if a test exists. The SDOC shall be enhanced as follows:

For Part 1, General Requirements:

> The **object of the declaration** is identified by the product hardware, software or hardware and software combination, revision level and release date.
>
> The **document requiring conformity** is this USGv6 Profile document, version and date.
>
> **Additional information** shall include an enumeration of the Host, Router or Network Protection Device functional categories and configuration options specified in this profile, for which compliance is being claimed.

For Part 2, Supporting Documentation:

> The chain of traceability requires that conformity assessment results be made available to purchasers for:
> - Conformance and Interoperability, in the case of Hosts and Routers, and
> - Functional testing, in the case of Network Protection Devices.
>
> These results shall be traceable to NIST SP-500-273 IPv6 Test Methods: General Description and Validation, used in accredited testing laboratories. Each such testing laboratory shall be accredited by a body which is signatory to the International Laboratory Accreditation Cooperation (ILAC).

8. USGv6-V1 Node Requirements Table

The Node Requirements Table in this section is the normative, definitive specification of requirements for IPv6 Host, Routers and NPDs that claim compliance to this profile. Section 6 of this document provides informative discussion and interpretation of the requirements embodied in this table. Should the requirements as described in section 6 differ from the requirements specified in this table, the table will take precedent.

The requirements in the table are grouped into the same functional categories as described in section 1.3.3. In general, this is just a matter of convenience and presentation and the grouping of requirements into functional categories has no impact on the normativity of individual requirements.

The table primarily consists of a list of identified public specifications (e.g., IETF RFCs). The Spec/Reference column of the table contains the document number of the most recent version of each specification cited. If available, this column also contains URLs to an online version of the specification. A (potentially abbreviated) Title of the specification is provided. The notational conventions of the table are to bold a RFC title when it is a principal, or compendium, specification under the Functional Category. Subsidiary RFCs and sections are not bolded. Where RFCs embody simple enhancements to other RFCs, they are right justified similar to section references. Where a specific detail within a specification is identified, this is listed by its Section number. RFC requirements unique to this profile are flagged with a * in the section column.

Each specification has a Status and Year of publication. In the case of RFCs the status of the document, including PS (Proposed Standard) and DS (Draft Standard) is determined by its maturity on the standards track. This is specified by *Internet Standards Process – Revision 3* [RFC2026]. The status levels exclusively refer to a specification's position in the IETF standards process.

The table provides for distinct requirements to be expressed in the Hosts, Routers and NPDs columns These columns express the requirement level of each specification and subsection cited. The terminology used to designate this, including MUST, SHOULD, MAY, are given in *Key Words for Use in RFCs to Indicate Requirement Levels* [RFC2119]. In this table we abbreviate MUST with "M", SHOULD with "S", SHOULD+ with "S+", and Optional (same as MAY) with "O". Any provision marked SHOULD+ in this version of the profile is subject to strengthening to MUST in a future version.

The Condition/Context column captures the configuration options and scopes of applicability that affect the applicability of various requirements level. In general, an unqualified requirement level of M, S+, S, or O in a device column indicates an unconditional requirement. If there are entries in the condition/context column of such entries, they merely provide context clues as to the group of capabilities to which this requirement should be interpreted. For example many of the requirements for cryptographic algorithms provide context flags of "IKE", "ESP" or "AH" to indicate which protocols cite the specific algorithm.

Requirement levels that are truly conditional upon configuration options employ the notation: "c(X,Y)". This notation is to be understood as meaning: if the condition specified holds, then the requirement level is "X", otherwise the requirement level is "Y". We use the shorthand notation "c(X)" to denote a requirement in which, if the condition does not hold then the requirement level is "O". All requirements are implicitly "O" when no other explicit requirement is stated. Simple logical AND / OR functions are supported in the Condition column.

Examples of expressions of conditional requirement levels are given below.

Condition	Router	Meaning
DHCP-Prefix	c(M,S+)	If the configuration option DHCP-Prefix is selected then the requirement level is "M", otherwise it is "S+".
EGW or 6PE	c(M)	If either the EGW or 6PE configuration option is selected, the requirement level is "M", otherwise "O".

The profile configuration options are defined in the profile templates for Hosts (section 3), Routers (section 4) and Network Protection Devices (section 5). Note that these configuration options are specified independently for each class/instance of device (despite the fact that we use a single shared column to represent them).

Finally, the Effective Date column documents the earliest date at which devices should be required to document compliance with a given requirement. This date shall be set to follow the life cycle and compliance guidance given in sections 1.4 and 7.1.

Spec / Reference	Section	USGv6-V1 Node Requirements Title / Definition	Status	Year	Condition / Context	Host
		IPv6 Basic Requirements				
RFC2460		**IPv6 Specification**	DS	1998		M
	2	IPv6 Packets: send, receive				M
	2	IPv6 packet forwarding				
	4	Extension headers: processing				M
	4.3	Hop-by-Hop & unrecognized options				M
	4.5	Fragment headers: send, receive, process				M
	4.6	Destination Options extensions				M
RFC5095		**Deprecation of Type 0 Routing Headers**	PS	2007		M
RFC2711		**IPv6 Router Alert Option**	PS	1999		
RFC4443		**ICMPv6**	DS	2006		M
RFC4884		**Extended ICMP for Multi-Part Messages**	PS	2007		S+
RFC1981		**Path MTU Discovery for IPv6**	DS	1996		M
	4	Discovery Protocol Requirements				M
RFC2675		**IPv6 Jumbograms**	PS	1999		O
RFC4861		**Neighbor Discovery for IPv6**	DS	2006		M
	4.1, 4.2	Router Discovery				M
	4.6.2	Prefix Discovery				M
	7.2	Address Resolution				M
	7.2.5	NA and NS processing				M
(RFC4862)	7.2.3	Duplicate Address Detection				M
	7.3	Neighbor Unreachability Detection				M
	8	Redirect functionality				S
RFC5175		**IPv6 Router Advertisement Flags Option**	PS	2008		S
RFC4191		**Default Router Preference**	PS	2005		S+
RFC3971		**Secure Neighbor Discovery**	PS	2005	SEND	c(M)

Spec / Reference	Section	USGv6-V1 Node Requirements		Status	Year	Condition / Context	Hos
		Title / Definition					
		Auto Configuration					
RFC4862		**IPv6 Stateless Address Autoconfig**		DS	2007	SLAAC	c(M
	5.3	Creation of Link Local Addresses				SLAAC	**M**
(RFC4861)	5.4	Duplicate Address Detection				SLAAC	**M**
	5.5	Creation of Global Addresses				SLAAC	c(M
	*	Ability to Disable Creation of Global Addrs				SLAAC	c(M
RFC4941		**Privacy Extensions for IPv6 SLAAC**		PS	2001	SLAAC & PriAddr	c(M
	*	<2nd context for MIP Mobile Node>				SLAAC & MIP	c(S-
RFC3736		**Stateless DHCP Service for IPv6**		PS	2004	SLAAC	c(S-
RFC3315		**Dynamic Host Config Protocol (DHCPv6)**		PS	2003	DHCP-Client	c(M
	*	Ability to Administratively Disable				DHCP-Client	c(M
		DHCP Client Functions				DHCP-Client	c(M
RFC4361		**Node-specific Client IDs for DHCPv4**		PS	2006	DHCP-Client & IPv4	c(S-
RFC3633		**Prefix Delegation**		PS	2003	DHCP-Prefix	
		Addressing Requirements					
RFC4291		**IPv6 Addressing Architecture**		DS	2006		**M**
RFC4007		IPv6 Scoped Address Architecture		PS	2005		**M**
-	*	Ability to manually configure Addresses					**M**
RFC4193		Unique Local IPv6 Unicast Address		PS	2005		O
RFC3879		Deprecating Site Local Addresses		PS	2004		**M**
RFC3484		Default Address Selection for IPv6		PS	2003		**M**
	2.1	Configurable Selection Policies					S+
RFC2526		Reserved IPv6 Subnet Anycast Addresses		PS	1999		**M**
RFC3972		**Cryptographically Generated Addresses**		PS	2005	SEND or CGA	c(M
RFC4581		(CGA) Extension Field Format		PS	2006	SEND or CGA	c(M
RFC4982		(CGA) Support for Multiple Hash Algos.		PS	2007	SEND or CGA	c(M

Spec / Reference	Section	USGv6-V1 Node Requirements Title / Definition	Status	Year	Condition / Context	Host
		Application Requirements				
RFC3596		**DNS Extensions for IPv6**	DS	2003	DNS-Client	c(M)
	2.1	Support of AAAA records			DNS-Client	c(M)
	2.5	Support of ipv6.arpa PTR records			DNS-Client	c(M)
RFC2671		**Extension Mechanisms for DNS (EDNS0)**	PS	199	DNS-Client	c(M)
RFC3226		**DNSSEC and IPv6 DNS MSG Size Reqs**	PS	2001	DNS-Client	c(M)
RFC3986		**URI: Generic Syntax**	S-66	2005	URI	c(M)
RFC3493		**Basic Socket API for IPv6**	INF	2003	SOCK	c(M)
RFC3542		Advanced Socket API for IPv6	INF	2003	SOCK & MIP	c(M)
RFC4584		Extension to Sockets API for Mobile IPv6	INF	2006	SOCK & MIP	c(M)
RFC3678		Socket API Extensions Multicast Source Filters	INF	2004	SOCK & SSM	c(M)
RFC5014		Socket API for Source Address Selection	INF	2007	SOCK	c(S+)
		Specific Applications				
RFC3596		DNS Server Functions	DS	2003	DNS-Server	c(M)
RFC3315		DHCPv6 Server Functions	PS	2003	DHCP-Server	c(M)
		Routing Protocol Requirements				
		Interior Routing Protocol				
RFC2740		**OSPF for IPv6**	PS	1999	IGW	
RFC4552		Authentication/Confidentiality for OSPFv3	PS	2006	IGW	
		Exterior Routing Protocol				
RFC4271		**Border Gateway Protocol 4 (BGP-4)**	DS	2006	EGW or 6PE	
RFC1772		BGP Application in the Internet	DS	1995	EGW or 6PE	
RFC4760		BGP Multi-Protocol Extensions	DS	2007	EGW or 6PE	
RFC2545		BGP Multi-Protocol Extensions for IPv6 IDR	PS	1999	EGW or 6PE	

Spec / Reference	Section	USGv6-V1 Node Requirements Title / Definition	Status	Year	Condition / Context	Hos
		IP Security Requirements				
		IPsec-v3				
RFC4301		**Security Architecture for the IP**	PS	2005		M
-	4.1	Support of Transport Mode SAs			IGW or IPv4	M
-	4.5.1	Manual SA and Key Management				M
-	4.5.2	Automated SA and Key Management				M
RFC4303		Encapsulating Security Payload (ESP)	PS	2005	IPsec-v3	M
RFC4302		Authentication Header (AH)	PS	2005	IPsec-v3	O
RFC3948		UDP Encapsulation of ESP Packets	PS	2005	IPsec-v3	O
-						
RFC4835		Cryptographic Algorithms for ESP and AH	PS	2007	IPsec-v3	M
-	*	(See additional 4835 requirements below)				
RFC4308		Cryptographic Suites for IPsec	PS	2005	IPsec-v3	O
	2.1	VPN-A			IPsec-v3	S
	2.2	VPN-B			IPsec-v3	S+
RFC4869		Suite B Cryptographic Suites for IPsec	INF	2007	IPsec-v3	O
RFC4809		Requirements for an IPsec Cert Mgmt Profile	INF	2007	IPsec-v3	S+
-						
		IKEv2				
RFC4306		**Internet Key Exchange (IKEv2) Protocol**	PS	2005	IKEv2	M
	4	Pre-shared secrets for peer authentication			IKEv2	M
	4	RSA sig auth			IKEv2	M
	4	NAT-T in IKEv2			IKEv2	O
	3.3.3	ESN			IKEv2	M
RFC4718		IKEv2 Clarifications & Impl. Guidelines	INF	2006	IKEv2	S
RFC4307		Cryptographic Algorithms for IKEv2	PS	2005	IKEv2	M
-		(See additional 4307 requirements below)				
RFC3526		More MODP DH Groups for IKE	PS	2003	IKEv2	S
RFC5114		Additional DH Groups for Use with IETF Stds	INF	2008	IKEv2	O
-	2.3.3.2	Diffie-Hellman MODP group 24			IKEv2	M
-						
RFC4945		Internet IPsec PKI Profile of IKEv1, IKEv2 & PKIX	PS	2007	IKEv2	S+

Spec / Reference	Section	USGv6-V1 Node Requirements Title / Definition	Status	Year	Condition / Context	Host
		Uses of Cryptographic Algorithms				
RFC2410		NULL Encryption	PS	1998		M
RFC4835	3.1.1	NULL Encryption			ESP	M
RFC2451		ESP CBC-mode Algorithms	PS	1998		M
	2.6	3DES-CBC			ESP	M
RFC4835	3.1.1	3DES-CBC			ESP	M
RFC4307	3.1.1	3DES-CBC			IKEv2	M
RFC3602		AES-CBC	PS	2003		M
RFC4835	3.1.1	AES-CBC with 128 bit keys			ESP	M
RFC4307	3.1.1	AES-CBC with 128 bit keys			IKEv2	M
RFC3686		AES-CTR	PS	2004		S
RFC4835	3.1.1	AES-CTR with 128-bit keys			ESP	S
RFC4307	3.1.3	AES-CTR with 128-bit keys			IKEv2	S
RFC4309		AES-CCM	PS	2005		O
RFC4835	3.1.2	AES-CCM with 128 bit keys			ESP	O
RFC4106		AES-GCM	PS	2005		O
	6	128-bit ICV			ESP	O
	8.1	AES-GCM with 128 bit keys			ESP	O
RFC4543		AES-GMAC	PS	2006		O
	5.4	ENCR-NULL-AUTH-AES-GMAC 128 bit keys			ESP	O
	5.4	AUTH-AES-GMAC with 128 bit keys			AH	O
RFC2404		HMAC-SHA-1-96	PS	1998		M
RFC4835	3.1.1/3.2	HMAC-SHA-1			ESP or AH	M
RFC4307	3.1.1	HMAC-SHA-1			IKEv2	M
RFC4307	3.1.4	HMAC-SHA-1 as a PRF			IKEv2	M
RFC4868		HMAC-SHA-256	PS	2007		S+
-	2.3	HMAC-SHA-256-128			ESP or AH	S+
-	2.3	HMAC-SHA-256-128			IKEv2	S+
-	2.4	HMAC-SHA-256 as a PRF			IKEv2	S+
RFC3566		AES-XCBC-MAC-96	PS	2003		S+
RFC4835	3.1.1/3.2	AES-XCBC-MAC-96			ESP or AH	S+
RFC4307	3.1.5	AES-XCBC-MAC-96			IKEv2	S+
RFC4434		AES-XCBC-PRF-128	PS	2006		S+
RFC4307	3.1.4	AES128-XCBC-PRF			IKEv2	S+

Spec / Reference	Section	USGv6-V1 Node Requirements Title / Definition	Status	Year	Condition / Context	Hos
		Transition Mechanisms Requirements				
RFC4038		**Application Aspects of IPv6 Transition**	INF	2005	IPv4	S
RFC4213		**Transition Mech. for Hosts & Routers**	PS	2005	IPv4	c(M
	2	Dual Stack IPv4 and IPv6			IPv4	c(M
	3	Configured Tunnels			IPv4	c(S)
RFC4891		Using IPsec to Secure IPv6-in-IPv4 Tunnels	INF	2007	IPv4	c(S)
RFC2473		Generic Packet Tunneling in IPv6	PS	1998	IPv4	
RFC2784		Generic Routing Encapsulation	PS	2000	IPv4	
		IPv6 Provider Edge MPLS Tunneling				
RFC4798		Connecting IPv6 islands over IPv4 MPLS (6PE)	PS	2007	IPv4 & 6PE	
		Network Management Requirements				
RFC3411		**SNMP v3 Management Framework**	S62	2002	SNMP	c(M
RFC3412		SNMP Message Process and Dispatch	S62	2002	SNMP	c(M
RFC3413		SNMP Applications	S62	2002	SNMP	c(M
	1.2	Command Responder			SNMP	c(M
	1.3	Notification Generator			SNMP	c(S)
RFC3414		User-based Security Model for SNMPv3	S62	2002	SNMP	c(M
		Management Information Bases				
RFC4293		MIB for the IP	PS	2006	SNMP	c(M
RFC4292		MIB for IP Forwarding Table	PS	2006	SNMP	
RFC4022		MIB for TCP	PS	2006	SNMP	c(S+
RFC4113		MIB for UDP	PS	2005	SNMP	c(S+
RFC4087		MIB for IP Tunnels	PS	2005	SNMP & IPv4	
RFC4807		MIB for IPsec Policy Database Configuration	PS	2007	SNMP & IPsec-v3	
RFC4295		MIB for Mobile IP	PS	2006	SNMP & MIP	
RFC3289		MIB for DiffServ	PS	2002	SNMP & DS	

Spec / Reference	Section	USGv6-V1 Node Requirements Title / Definition	Status	Year	Condition / Context	Host
		Multicast Requirements				
RFC3810		**MLD Version 2 for IPv6**	PS	2004		**M**
RFC3306		**Unicast-Prefix-based IPv6 Mcast Addresses**	PS	2002		**M**
RFC3307		**Allocation Guidelines for IPv6 Mcast Addrs**	PS	2002		**M**
RFC4607		**Source-Specific Multicast for IP**	PS	2006	SSM	c(M)
RFC4604		MLDv2 for Source Specific Multicast (SSM)	PS	2006	SSM	c(M)
		Protocol Independent Multicast (PIM)				
RFC4601		PIM Sparse Mode (SM)	PS	2006	SSM	
RFC4609		PIM-SM Security Issues / Enhancements	INF	2006	SSS	
RFC3956		Embedding Rendezvous Point (RP) Mcast Addr	PS	2004	SSM	
		Mobility Requirements				
RFC3775		**Mobility Support in IPv6**	PS	2004	MIP	c(M)
	8.1	All Nodes as Correspondent Node			MIP	**M**
	8.2	Route Optimization			MIP	c(M)
	8.2	Allow route optimization to be disabled.			MIP	c(M)
	8.3	All IPv6 Routers			MIP	
	8.4	Home Agents			MIP	
	8.5	Mobile Nodes			MIP	c(M)
RFC4282		The Network Access Identifier	PS	2005	MIP	c(S+)
RFC4283		Mobile Node Identifier option for MIPV6	PS	2005	MIP	c(S+)
RFC4877		MIPv6 Op with IKEv2 and Revised IPsec Arch	PS	2004	MIP	c(M)
RFC3963		Network Mobility (NEMO) Basic Support	PS	2005	NEMO	
		Quality of Service Requirements				
RFC2474		**Differentiated Services (DiffServ)**	PS	1988	DS	c(M)
RFC2475		An Architecture for Differentiated Services	INF	1998	DS	
RFC3260		New Terminology / Clarifications for Diffserv	INF	2002	DS	
RFC2983		Differentiated Services and Tunnels	INF	2000	DS	
RFC4594		Config Guidelines for DS Service Classes	INF	2006	DS	
RFC3086		Def. of DiffServe Per Domain Behaviors (PDB)	INF	2001	DS	
RFC3140		Per Hop Behavior (PHB) Identification Codes	PS	2001	DS	c(M)
RFC2597		Assured Forwarding PHB Group	PS	1999	DS	
RFC3246		An Expedited Forwarding PHB	PS	2002	DS	
RFC3247		Supplemental Info for the New EF PHB	INF	2002	DS	
RFC3168		**Explicit Congestion Notification (ECN) to IP**	PS	2001	ECN	S

Spec / Reference	Section	USGv6-V1 Node Requirements / Title / Definition	Status	Year	Condition / Context	Ho
		Link Specific Requirements				
RFC2464		IPv6 over Ethernet	PS	1998	Link	c(
RFC2467		IPv6 over FDDI	PS	1998	Link	c(
RFC5072		IPv6 over PPP	PS	1998	Link	c(
RFC2491		IPv6 over Non-Broadcast Multiple Access (NBMA) networks	PS	1999	Link	c(
RFC2492		IPv6 over ATM Networks	PS	1999	Link	c(
RFC2497		IPv6 over ARCnet	PS	1999	Link	c(
RFC2590		IPv6 over Frame Relay	PS	1999	Link	c(
RFC3146		IPv6 over IEEE 1394 Networks	PS	2001	Link	c(
RFC3572		IPv6 over MAPOS (SONET/SDH)	INF	2003	Link	c(
RFC4338		IPv6 & IPv4 over Fibre Channel	PS	2006	Link	c(
RFC4944		IPv6 over IEEE 802.15.4 Networks	PS	2007	Link	c(
		Packet Compression Technologies				
RFC2507		IP Header Compression	PS	1999		(
RFC3173		IP Payload Compression Protocol (IPComp)	PS	2001		(
RFC4995		RObust Header Compression (ROHC) Framework	PS	2007	ROHC	c(
RFC4996		ROHC Profile for TCP	PS	2007	ROHC	c(
RFC3095		ROHC Profiles for RTP, UDP, ESP and Uncomp	PS	2001	ROHC	c(
RFC4815		Corrections and Clarifications to RFC3095	PS	2007	ROHC	c(
RFC3843		ROHC Profile for IP Only	PS	2004	ROHC	c(:
RFC3241		ROHC over PPP	PS	2002	ROHC & Link	c(
RFC4362		ROHC: Link Assisted for IP/UDP/RTP	PS	2006	ROHC	c(:

Spec / Reference	Section	USGv6-V1 Node Requirements			Condition /	
		Title / Definition	Status	Year	Context	Host
		Network Protection Device Requirements				
SP500-267	6.12.3.1	IPv6 connectivity			NPD	
SP500-267	6.12.3.2	Dual Stack			NPD	
SP500-267	6.12.3.3	Administrative Functionality			NPD	
SP500-267	6.12.3.4	Authentication and Authorization			NPD	
SP500-267	6.12.3.5	Security of Control and Comms			NPD	
SP500-267	6.12.3.6	Persistence			NPD	
SP500-267	6.12.3.7	Logging and Alerts			NPD	
SP500-267	6.12.3.8	Fragmented Packets Handling			NPD	
SP500-267	6.12.3.9	Tunneled Traffic Handling			NPD	
SP500-267	6.12.4.1.1	Port/protocol/address blocking			FW or APFW	
SP500-267	6.12.4.1.2	Asymmetrical Blocking			FW or APFW	
SP500-267	6.12.4.1.3	IPsec Traffic Handling			FW or APFW	
SP500-267	6.12.4.1.4	Performance Under Load, Fail Safe			FW or APFW	
SP500-267	6.12.4.2.1	No violation of trust barriers			APFW	
SP500-267	6.12.4.2.2	Session Traffic Auth			APFW	
SP500-267	6.12.4.2.3	Email, File Filtering			APFW	
SP500-267	6.12.5.1.1	Known Attack Detection			IDS or IPS	
SP500-267	6.12.5.1.2	Malformed pkt detection			IDS or IPS	
SP500-267	6.12.5.1.3	Port scan detection			IDS or IPS	
SP500-267	6.12.5.1.4	Tunneled traffic detection			IDS or IPS	
SP500-267	6.12.5.1.5	Logging and Alerts			IDS or IPS	
SP500-267	6.12.5.1.6	Performance Under Load, Fail Safe			IDS or IPS	
SP500-267	6.12.5.2.1	Intrusion Prevention			IPS	

Appendix A—Profile Usage Guidance & Examples

This appendix provides guidance on the expected usage scenarios for this profile. As noted in section 1.1 and 1.2 this profile is intended to be a strategic planning document for USG IT planning and acquisition officials that provides a technical basis for conveying technical requirements to IPv6 product vendors. As such, its primary value is in identifying and documenting sets of technical requirements for IPv6 capabilities in common network products.

It is important to recognize that the profile is not meant to provide deployment or operational guidance for the use of IPv6 in Federal networks. Other documents and efforts will have to address these issues. Instead the only purpose of the profile is to allow its users to describe the required IPv6 capabilities of network products that must be correctly implemented and available for acquisition.

The profile selects and organizes requirements (section 1.3) based upon device types (section 1.3.2) and functional categories capabilities (section 1.3.3) and defines requirement levels (section 1.3.1) for each set of requirements. Using these basic documentation techniques, the profile presents its user with individual profile templates (section 1.3.4) for Hosts (section 3), Routers (section 4) and Network Protection Devices (section 5). The end result is that the user is provided a template that defines a set of mandatory requirements and selectable configuration options for each device type. Section 6 of the profile discusses the logic of the decision process that determined which capabilities were made mandatory (MUSTs) and which capabilities were made optional (SHOULD+, SHOULD, MAY).

The Node Requirements Table (NRT) of section 8 provides the definitive tabular summary of technical requirements for each device type and configuration option. This table is organized by standard specification (RFC) and indicates the requirement levels for each RFC (and sub-function) relative to each device type and configuration option.

The profile defines the notation *device-type:* USGv6-V1-Capable to describe the set of unconditionally mandatory requirements for the specified device type (i.e., bold **M**s in the NRT). In a fully specified set of requirements for a given product, *device-type:* USGv6-V1-Capable defines the base set of requirements common to every device of that type. It should be noted that for a given device type, these base sets include some capabilities that are given specific context names in the NRT, or that are conditional for other device types. In particular, for both Hosts and Routers, the set USGv6-V1-Capable includes the unconditional MUSTs identified by the IPsec-V3, IKEv2, ESP and AH contexts. Likewise Router: USGv6-V1-Capable implicitly contains the unconditional MUSTs associated with the SNMP and DS context/conditions.

The selection of each configuration option adds to the set of mandatory requirements for a specific product. The profile uses a "+" notation to indicate the addition of each set of mandatory requirements associated with each configuration option. Thus the notation Host: USGv6-V1-Capable +SLAAC defines the set of Host requirements that are unconditionally mandatory along with those mandatory requirements defined for Stateless Address Auto Configuration capabilities.

It is expected that users of this profile will use the device profile templates in sections 3, 4, and 5 to chose and document IPv6 capability requirements for specific procurements. The USGv6 Capabilities Checklist below provides another way to summarize and document the IPv6 requirements for and capabilities of individual products. The checklist summarizes the configuration options and contexts for each device type. In addition, the checklist flags (with bold **M**s) those functional categories that contain unconditional MUSTs. Consult the Node Requirements Table for the detailed list of specific requirements associated with configuration option and those that are unconditional requirements.

Spec / Reference	Section	USGv6-V1 Capability Check List / IPv6 Requirements	Configuration Option	Host	Router	NPD	Notes
		Note: Gray check boxes imply an atypical selection for device type. See profile text for details.					
		Note: **M** indicates category/context contains unconditional mandatory requirements. See NRT for details.					
SP500-267	6.1	**IPv6 Basic Requirements**		M	M		
		support of stateless address auto-configuration	SLAAC				Host:[O:1]
		support of SLAAC privacy extensions.	PrivAddr				Host:[O:1]
		support of stateful (DHCP) address auto-configuration	DHCP-Client				
		support of automated router prefix delegation	DHCP-Prefix				
		support of neighbor discovery security extensions	SEND				
SP500-267	6.6	**Addressing Requirements**		M	M		
		support of cryptographically generated addresses	CGA				
SP500-267	6.7	**IP Security Requirements**		M	M		
		support of the IP security architecture	IPsec-V3	M	M		
		support for automated key management	IKEv2	M	M		
		support for encapsulating security payloads in IP	ESP	M	M		
SP500-267	6.11	**Application Requirements**					
		support of DNS client/resolver functions	DNS-Client				
		support of Socket application program interfaces	SOCK				
		support of IPv6 uniform resource identifiers	URI				
		support of a DNS server application	DNS-Sever				
		support of a DHCP server application	DHCP-Server				
SP500-267	6.2	**Routing Protocol Requirements**					
		support of the intra-domain (interior) routing protocols	IGW				
		support for inter-domain (exterior) routing protocols	EGW				
SP500-267	6.4	**Transition Mechanism Requirements**					
		support of interoperation with IPv4-only systems	IPv4				
		support of tunneling IPv6 over IPv4 MPLS services	6PE				
SP500-267	6.8	**Network Management Requirements**			M		
		support of network management services	SNMP		M		
SP500-267	6.9	**Multicast Requirements**		M	M		
		full support of multicast communications	SSM				
SP500-267	6.10	**Mobility Requirements**					
		support of mobile IP capability.	MIP				
		support of mobile network capabilities	NEMO				
SP500-267	6.3	**Quality of Service Requirements**			M		
		support of Differentiated Services capabilities	DS		M		
SP500-267	6.12	**Network Protection Device Requirements**				M	
		support of basic firewall capabilities	FW				NPD:[O:1]
		support of application firewall capabilities	APFW				NPD:[O:1]
		support of intrusion detection capabilities	IDS				NPD:[O:1]
		support of intrusion protection capabilities	IPS				NPD:[O:1]
SP500-267	6.5	**Link Specific Technologies**		M	M		
		support of robust packet compression services	ROHC				
		support of link technology	Link=	M	M		[O:1]
		(repeat as needed) support of link technology	Link=				

Using the configuration options, users of the profile can specify distinct sets of requirements for various classes/types of products. In what follows, we provide some examples of what might be typical uses of the templates.

- A typical personal computer acquisition specification can be expressed by requiring demonstrated compliance to:

  o **Host: USGv6-V1-Capable+IPv4+DHCP-client+DNS-Client+ URI+Link=Ethernet.**

  o This describes a basic dual-stacked host system with an Ethernet interface and supporting DHCP address auto configuration and IPv6 enabled DNS and URI capabilities.

- A typical mobility enabled laptop acquisition specification can be expressed by requiring demonstrated compliance to:

  o **Host: USGv6-V1-Capable+DHCP-client+DNS-Client+ URI+MIP+Link=Ethernet+LINK=PPP+ROHC**

  o This describes a host system similar to the one above, but with the ability to be a MIP mobile node and with additional an additional interface supporting PPP with robust header compression capabilities. Note that this system is not required to support IPv4 interoperability / transition mechanisms. This system can be IPv6-only as far as these requirements are concerned.

- A typical Unix[11] server acquisition specification can be expressed as requiring demonstrated compliance to:

  o **Host: USGv6-V1-Capable+IPv4+DHCP-Client+URI+SOCK+DNS-Client+ Link=Ethernet.**

  Note: SOCK – MUST support RFC3542 Advance Socket API for IPv6.

  o This describes a dual stacked Unix server with support for "C" socket APIs and enhances the profile's requirements by mandating support for an additional API that the profile leaves as optional.

- The simplest IPv6 enabled node (e.g., embedded system, etc.) might be specified as:

  o **Host: USGv6-V1-Capable+SLAAC+ Link=Ethernet**

  o This describes a minimal IPv6 enabled system, supporting stateless address auto-configuration and an Ethernet interface.

- A typical enterprise intra-net router acquisition specification can be expressed as requiring demonstrated compliance to:

  o **Router: USGv6-V1-Capable+IGW+IPv4+Link=Ethernet**

---

[11] Unix® is a registered trademark of The Open Group.

- o This describes a dual-stacked interior gateway, running OSPF over Ethernet interfaces.

- A more capable intra-net router, requiring support for source specific multicast routing, support for mobile IP home agent capabilities and specific QoS capabilities might be specified as follows:

  - o **Router: USGv6-V1-Capable+IGW+IPv4+MIP+SSM+Link=Ethernet**

    Note: DS – MUST support of Expedited Forwarding PHB (RFC3246 and RFC3247).

  - o This describes an enhanced interior router that modifies the profile requirements by mandating support for the Expedited Forwarding per hop behavior as a specific implementation of Differentiated Services QoS.

- A typical customer premise stub router acquisition specification would be expressed as requiring demonstrated compliance to:

  - o **Router: USGv6-V1-Capable+DHCP-Prefix+DHCP-Client +Link=Ethernet**

  - o This describes a simple CPE stub router with Ethernet interfaces that is capable of being configured through DHCP by an upstream ISP router.

- A typical enterprise Internet border router acquisition specification would be expressed as requiring demonstrated compliance to:

  - o **Router: USGv6-V1-Capable+EGW+IGW+IPv4+6PE +Link=Ethernet+Link=MAPOS**

  - o This describes a dual-stacked exterior gateway, running BGP on external SONET interfaces and OSPF over interior Ethernet interfaces. The requirements include support of dual-stack and configured tunnel transition mechanism and support of IPv6 over IPv4 MPLS tunnels.

- A typical enterprise firewall acquisition specification would be expressed as requiring demonstrated compliance to:

  - o **NPD: FW+AFW** and **Router: USGv6-V1-Capable+IGW+Link=Ethernet**

  - o This describes a hybrid device that acts as both a basic and application firewall coupled to with simple interior gateway capabilities. Note it would be up to the user to specify any deviations that the hybrid device may have relative to the base IGW specification.

- A typical Intrusion Detection and Prevention system would be expressed as requiring demonstrated compliance to:

  - o **NPD: IDS+IPS**

  - o This describes only the IDS and IPS capabilities required of the system.

By providing a convenient way to select and articulate sets of requirements, the profile facilitates the description of a vast array of distinct product configurations / classes. While we suspect that there will be a few bundled sets of requirements that will be used quite commonly, we also believe that there is tremendous variance in the packaging of feature sets in commercial products and attempts to overly "standardize" such configurations may not afford the flexibility needed.

Appendix B—Bibliography and References

[1] RFC1752 *the Recommendation for the IP Next Generation Protocol*. S. Bradner, A. Mankin. January 1995.

[2] RFC1772 *Application of the Border Gateway Protocol in the Internet*, Y. Rekhter and P. Gross, March 1995.

[3] RFC1981 *Path MTU Discovery for IPv6*, J. McCann, S. Deering and J. Mogul, August 1996.

[4] RFC1997 *BGP Communities Attribute*, R. Chandra, P. Traina and T. Li, Proposed Standard, August 1996.

[5] RFC2026 *The Internet Standards Process -- Revision 3*. S. Bradner. October 1996.

[6] RFC2119 *Key words for use in RFCs to Indicate Requirement Levels*. S. Bradner. March 1997.

[7] RFC2185 *Routing Aspects of IPv6 Transition* R. Callon, D. Haskin September 1997.

[8] RFC2401 *Security Architecture for the Internet Protocol* S. Kent, R. Atkinson November 1998.

[9] RFC2402 *IP Authentication Header* S. Kent, R. Atkinson November 1998.

[10] RFC2404 *The Use of HMAC-SHA-1-96 within ESP and AH*, C. Madson, R. Glenn, November 1998.

[11] RFC2406 *IP Encapsulating Security Payload (ESP)* S. Kent, R. Atkinson November 1998.

[12] RFC2410 *The NULL Encryption Algorithm and Its Use With IPsec*. R. Glenn, S. Kent. November 1998

[13] RFC2451 The *ESP CBC-Mode Cipher Algorithms*. R. Pereira, R. Adams. November 1998

[14] RFC2460 *Internet Protocol Version 6 (IPv6) Specification*. S. Deering, R. Hinden. December 1998.

[15] RFC2464 *Transmission of IPv6 Packets over Ethernet Networks* M. Crawford December 1998.

[16] RFC2467 *Transmission of IPv6 Packets over FDDI Networks* M. Crawford December 1998.

[17] RFC2473 *Generic Packet Tunneling in IPv6*, Conta A and Deering S, December 1998.

[18] RFC2474 *Definition of the Differentiated Services Field in the IPv4 and IPv6 Headers*, K. Nichols, S. Blake, F. Baker, D. Black, December 1998.

[19] RFC2475 *An Architecture for Differentiated Service* S. Blake, D. Black, M. Carlson, E. Davies, Z. Wang, W. Weiss December 1998.

[20] RFC2491 *IPv6 over Non-Broadcast Multiple Access (NBMA) networks* G. Armitage, P. Schulter, M. Jork, G. Harter January 1999.

[21] RFC2492 *IPv6 over ATM Networks* G. Armitage, P. Schulter, M. Jork January 1999.

[22] RFC2497 *Transmission of IPv6 Packets over ARCnet Networks* I. Souvatzis January 1999.

[23] RFC2507 *IP Header Compression* M. Degermark, B. Nordgren, S. Pink February 1999.

[24] RFC2526 *Reserved IPv6 Subnet Anycast Addresses*, D. Johnson and S. Deering, March 1999.

[25] RFC2545 *Use of BGP-4 Multiprotocol Extensions for IPv6 Inter-Domain Routing*, P. Marques, F. Dupont, March 1999.

[26] RFC2590 *Transmission of IPv6 Packets over Frame Relay Networks Specification* A. Conta, A. Malis, M. Mueller May 1999

[27] RFC2597 *Assured Forwarding PHB Group* J. Heinanen, F. Baker, W. Weiss, J. Wroclawski June 1999.

[28] RFC2671 *Extension Mechanisms for DNS (EDNS0)*. P. Vixie. August 1999

[29] RFC2675 *IPv6 Jumbograms*. D. Borman, S. Deering, R. Hinden. August 1999. Obsoletes RFC2147

[30] RFC2711 *IPv6 Router Alert Option*. C. Partridge, A. Jackson. October 1999

[31] RFC2740 *OSPF for IPv6*, R. Coltun, D. Ferguson and J. Moy. December 1999.

[32] RFC2784 *Generic Routing Encapsulation (GRE)* D. Farinacci, T. Li, S. Hanks, D. Meyer, P. Traina March 2000

[33] RFC2918 *Route Refresh Capability for BGP-4*, E. Chen, Proposed Standard, September 2000.

[34] RFC2983 *Differentiated Services and Tunnels* D. Black October 2000.

[35] RFC3086 *Definition of Differentiated Services Per Domain Behaviors and Rules for their Specification* K. Nichols, B. Carpenter April 2001.

[36] RFC3095 *RObust Header Compression (ROHC): Framework and four profiles: RTP, UDP, ESP, and uncompressed* C. Bormann, C. Burmeister, M. Degermark, H. Fukushima, H. Hannu, L-E. Jonsson, R. Hakenberg, T. Koren, K. Le, Z. Liu, A. Martensson, A. Miyazaki, K. Svanbro, T. Wiebke, T. Yoshimura, H. Zheng July 2001.

[37] RFC3140 *Per Hop Behavior Identification Codes* D. Black, S. Brim, B. Carpenter, F. Le Faucheur June 2001.

[38] RFC3146 *Transmission of IPv6 Packets over IEEE 1394 Networks* K. Fujisawa, A. Onoe October 2001

[39] RFC3168 *The Addition of Explicit Congestion Notification (ECN) to IP* K. Ramakrishnan, S. Floyd, D. Black September 2001.

[40] RFC3173 *IP Payload Compression Protocol (IPComp)* A. Shacham, B. Monsour, R. Pereira, M. Thomas September 2001.

[41] RFC3226 *DNSSEC and IPv6 A6 aware server/resolver message size requirements,* O. Gudmundsson, December 2001.

[42] RFC3241 *Robust Header Compression (ROHC) over PPP* C. Bormann April 2002.

[43] RFC3246 *An Expedited Forwarding PHB (Per-Hop Behavior)* B. Davie, A. Charny, J.C.R. Bennet, K. Benson, J.Y. Le Boudec, W. Courtney, S. Davari, V. Firoiu, D. Stiliadis March 2002.

[44] RFC3247 *Supplemental Information for the New Definition of the EF PHB (Expedited Forwarding Per-Hop Behavior)* A. Charny, J. Bennet, K. Benson, J. Boudec, A. Chiu, W. Courtney, S. Davari, V. Firoiu, C. Kalmanek, K. Ramakrishnan March 2002.

[45] RFC3260 *New Terminology and Clarifications for Diffserv* D. Grossman April 2002.

[46] RFC3289 *Management Information Base for the Differentiated Services Architecture* F. Baker, K. Chan, A. Smith May 2002

[47] RFC3306 *Unicast-Prefix-based IPv6 Multicast Addresses*, B. Haberman, D. Thaler, August 2002

[48] RFC3307 *Allocation Guidelines for IPv6 Multicast Addresses*, B. Haberman, August 2002

[49] RFC3315 *Dynamic Host Configuration Protocol for IPv6 (DHCPv6)*, R. Droms. Ed, J. Bound, B. Volz, T. Lemon, C. Perkins, M. Carney, July 2003.

[50] RFC3392 *Capabilities Advertisement with BGP-4*, R. Chandra, J. Scudder, Draft Standard, November 2002.

[51] RFC3411 *An Architecture for Describing Simple Network Management Protocol (SNMP) Management Frameworks.* D. Harrington, R. Presuhn, B. Wijnen. December 2002.

[52] RFC3412 *Message Processing and Dispatching for the Simple Network Management Protocol (SNMP)* J. Case, D. Harrington, R. Presuhn, B. Wijnen December 2002

[53] RFC3413 *SNMP Applications,* D. Levi, P. Meyer and B. Stewart, Standard, December 2002.

[54] RFC3414 *User-based Security Model (USM) for version 3 of the Simple Network Management Protocol (SNMPv3).* U. Blumenthal, B. Wijnen. December 2002.

[55] RFC3484 *Default Address Selection for Internet Protocol version 6 (IPv6).* R. Draves . February 2003

[56] RFC3493 *Basic Socket Interface Extensions for IPv6.* R. Gilligan, S. Thomson, J. Bound, J. McCann, W. Stevens. February 2003.

[57] RFC3526 *More Modular Exponential (MODP) Diffie-Hellman groups for Internet Key Exchange (IKE).* T. Kivinen, M. Kojo . May 2003

[58] RFC3542 *Advanced Sockets Application Program Interface (API) for IPv6.* W. Stevens, M. Thomas, E. Nordmark, T. Jinmei. May 2003.

[59] RFC3566 *The AES-XCBC-MAC-96 Algorithm and Its Use With IPsec* S. Frankel, H. Herbert September 2003.

[60] RFC3572 *Internet Protocol Version 6 over MAPOS (Multiple Access Protocol Over SONET/SDH)* T. Ogura, M. Maruyama, T. Yoshida July 2003

[61] RFC3596 *DNS Extensions to Support IP Version 6*. S. Thomson, C. Huitema, V. Ksinant, M. Souissi. October 2003.

[62] RFC3602 *The AES-CBC Cipher Algorithm and Its Use with IPsec*. S. Frankel, R. Glenn, S. Kelly. September 2003

[63] RFC3633 IPv6 *Prefix options for Dynamic Host Configuration Protocol (DHCP) version 6*, O. Troan and R. Droms, December 2003.

[64] RFC3678 *Socket Interface Extensions for Multicast Source Filters*. D. Thaler, B. Fenner, B. Quinn. January 2004.

[65] RFC3686 *Using Advanced Encryption Standard (AES) Counter Mode With IPsec Encapsulating Security Payload (ESP)*. R. Housley. January 2004

[66] RFC3736 *Stateless Dynamic Host Configuration Protocol (DHCP) Service for IPv6*. R. Droms. April 2004.

[67] RFC3750 *Unmanaged Networks IPv6 Transition Scenarios* C. Huitema, R. Austein, S. Satapati, R. van der Pol April 2004

[68] RFC3756 *IPv6 Neighbor Discovery (ND) Trust Models and Threats* P. Nikander, Ed., J. Kempf, E. Nordmark May 2004

[69] RFC3775 *Mobility Support in IPv6*. D. Johnson, C. Perkins, J. Arkko. June 2004.

[70] RFC3810 *Multicast Listener Discovery Version 2 (MLDv2) for IPv6*. R. Vida, Ed., L. Costa, Ed.. June 2004.

[71] RFC3843 *RObust Header Compression (ROHC): A Compression Profile for IP* L-E. Jonsson, G. Pelletier June 2004.

[72] RFC3879 *Deprecating Site Local Addresses*. C. Huitema, B. Carpenter. September 2004.

[73] RFC3904 *Evaluation of IPv6 Transition Mechanisms for Unmanaged Networks* C. Huitema, R. Austein, S. Satapati, R. van der Pol September 2004.

[74] RFC3948 *UDP Encapsulation of IPsec ESP Packets*. A. Huttunen, B. Swander, V. Volpe, L. DiBurro, M. Stenberg. January 2005.

[75] RFC3956 *Embedding the Rendezvous Point (RP) Address in an IPv6 Multicast Address,* P. Savola, B. Haberman November 2004.

[76] RFC3963 *Network Mobility (NEMO) Basic Support Protocol* V. Devarapalli, R. Wakikawa, A. Petrescu, P. Thubert January 2005

[77] RFC3971 *SEcure Neighbor Discovery*, J. Arkko (ed), J. Kempf, B. Zill, P. Nikander, March 2005.

[78] RFC3972 *Cryptographically Generated Addresses (CGA)*. T. Aura. March 2005

[79] RFC3986 *Uniform Resource Identifier (URI): Generic Syntax*. T. Berners-Lee, R. Fielding, L. Masinter. January 2005.

[80] RFC4007 *IPv6 Scoped Address Architecture*, S. Deering, B. Haberman, T. Jinmei, E. Nordmark, B. Zill, March 2005.

[81] RFC4022 *Management Information Base for the Transmission Control Protocol (TCP)* R. Raghunarayan, Ed. March 2005

[82] RFC4029 *Scenarios and Analysis for Introducing IPv6 into ISP Networks*, M. Lind, V. Ksinant, S. Park, A. Baudot, P. Savola, March 2005.

[83] RFC4038 *Application Aspects of IPv6 Transition* M-K. Shin, Ed., Y-G. Hong, J. Hagino, P. Savola, E. M. Castro March 2005.

[84] RFC4057 *IPv6 Enterprise Network Scenarios* J. Bound, Ed. June 2005.

[85] RFC4087 *IP Tunnel MIB* D. Thaler June 2005.

[86] RFC4106 *The Use of Galois/Counter Mode (GCM) in IPsec Encapsulating Security Payload (ESP)*. J. Viega, D. McGrew. June 2005.

[87] RFC4113 *Management Information Base for the User Datagram Protocol (UDP)* B. Fenner, J. Flick June 2005

[88] RFC4191 *Default Router Preferences and More-Specific Routes*. R. Draves, D. Thaler. November 2005

[89] RFC4193 *Unique Local IPv6 Unicast Addresses*, R. Hinden and B. Haberman, October 2005.

[90] RFC4213 *Basic Transition Mechanisms for IPv6 Hosts and Routers*, E. Nordmark and R. Gilligan, October 2005.

[91] RFC4271 *A Border Gateway Protocol 4 (BGP-4),* Y. Rekhter (ed), T. Li, S. Hares, January 2006.

[92] RFC4282 *The Network Access Identifier* B. Aboba, M. Beadles, J. Arkko, P. Eronen December 2005

[93] RFC4283 *Mobile Node Identifier Option for Mobile IPv6 (MIPv6)* A. Patel, K. Leung, M. Khalil, H. Akhtar, K. Chowdhury November 2005

[94] RFC4291 *IP Version 6 Addressing Architecture*, R. Hinden, S. Deering, February 2006.

[95] RFC4292 *IP Forwarding Table MIB* B. Haberman April 2006

[96] RFC4293 *Management Information Base for the Internet Protocol*, S. Routhier (ed), April 2006.

[97] RFC4294 *IPv6 Node Requirements*, Informational, J. Loughney (ed), April 2006.

[98] RFC4295 *Mobile IPv6 Management Information Base* G. Keeni, K. Koide, K. Nagami, S. Gundavelli April 2006.

[99] RFC4301 *Security Architecture for the Internet Protocol*, S. Kent and K. Seo, December 2005.

[100] RFC4302 *IP Authentication Header*, S. Kent, December 2005.

[101] RFC4303 *IP Encapsulating Security Payload (ESP),* S. Kent, December 2005.

[102] RFC4306 *Internet Key Exchange (IKEv2) Protocol*, C. Kaufman (ed), December 2005.

[103] RFC4307 *Cryptographic Algorithms for Use in the Internet Key Exchange Version 2 (IKEv2).* J. Schiller. December 2005.

[104] RFC4308 *Cryptographic Suites for IPsec*, P. Hoffman, December 2005.

[105] RFC4309 *Using Advanced Encryption Standard (AES) CCM Mode with IPsec Encapsulating Security Payload (ESP).* R. Housley December 2005.

[106] RFC4338 *Transmission of IPv6, IPv4, and Address Resolution Protocol (ARP) Packets over Fibre Channel* C. DeSanti, C. Carlson, R. Nixon January 2006

[107] RFC4360 *BGP Extended Communities Attribute*, S. Sangli, D. Tappan, Y. Rekhter, February 2006.

[108] RFC4361 *Node-specific Client Identifiers for Dynamic Host Configuration Protocol Version Four (DHCPv4).* T. Lemon, B. Sommerfeld. February 2006.

[109] RFC4362 *RObust Header Compression (ROHC): A Link-Layer Assisted Profile for IP/UDP/RTP* L-E. Jonsson, G. Pelletier, K. Sandlund January 2006

[110] RFC4434 *The AES-XCBC-PRF-128 Algorithm for the Internet Key Exchange Protocol (IKE)* P. Hoffman February 2006.

[111] RFC4443 *Internet Control Message Protocol (ICMPv6) for the Internet Protocol Version 6 (IPv6) Specification*, A. Conta, S. Deering, M. Gupta (ed), March 2006.

[112] RFC4472 *Operational Considerations and Issues with IPv6 DNS* A. Durand, J. Ihren, P. Savola April 2006

[113] RFC4543 *The Use of Galois Message Authentication Code (GMAC) in IPsec ESP and AH.* D. McGrew, J. Viega. May 2006.

[114] RFC4552 *Authentication/Confidentiality for OSPFv3.* M. Gupta, N. Melam. June 2006.

[115] RFC4554 *Use of VLANs for IPv4-IPv6 Coexistence in Enterprise Networks* T. Chown June 2006.

[116] RFC4581 *Cryptographically Generated Addresses (CGA) Extension Field Format.* Bagnulo, J. Arkko. October 2006.

[117] RFC4584 *Extension to Sockets API for Mobile IPv6.* S. Chakrabarti, E. Nordmark. July 2006.

[118] RFC4594 *Configuration Guidelines for DiffServ Service Classes* J. Babiarz, K. Chan, F. Baker August 2006

[119] RFC4601 *Protocol Independent Multicast - Sparse Mode (PIM-SM): Protocol Specification (Revised)* B. Fenner, M. Handley, H. Holbrook, I. Kouvelas August 2006

[120] RFC4604 *Using Internet Group Management Protocol Version 3 (IGMPv3) and Multicast Listener Discovery Protocol Version 2 (MLDv2) for Source-Specific Multicast.* H. Holbrook, B. Cain, B. Haberman. August 2006.

[121] RFC4607 *Source-Specific Multicast for IP* H. Holbrook, B. Cain August 2006.

[122] RFC4609 *Protocol Independent Multicast - Sparse Mode (PIM-SM) Multicast Routing Security Issues and Enhancements* P. Savola, R. Lehtonen, D. Meyer October 2006.

[123] RFC4718 *IKEv2 Clarifications and Implementation Guidelines* P. Eronen, P. Hoffman October 2006.

[124] RFC4760 *Dual Stack Multiprotocol BGP*, T. Bates, R. Chandra, D. Katz, Y. Rekhter, January 2007.

[125] RFC4798 *Connecting IPv6 Islands over IPv4 MPLS Using IPv6 Provider Edge Routers (6PE)*, J. De Clercq, D. Ooms, S. Prevost, F. Le Faucheur, February 2007.

[126] RFC4807 *IPsec Security Policy Database Configuration MIB* M. Baer, R. Charlet, W. Hardaker, R. Story, C. Wang March 2007

[127] RFC4809 *Requirements for an IPsec Certificate Management Profile*, C. Bonatti, S. Turner, G. Lebovitz, February 2007.

[128] RFC4815 *RObust Header Compression (ROHC): Corrections and Clarifications to RFC 3095* L-E. Jonsson, K. Sandlund, G. Pelletier, P. Kremer February 2007.

[129] RFC4835 *Cryptographic Algorithm Implementation Requirements for Encapsulating Security Payload (ESP) and Authentication Header (AH).* V. Manral, April 2007.

[130] RFC4852 *IPv6 Enterprise Network Analysis - IP Layer 3 Focus* J. Bound, Y. Pouffary, S. Klynsma, T. Chown, D. Green April 2007

[131] RFC4861 *Neighbor Discovery for IP version 6 (IPv6).* T. Narten, E. Nordmark, W. Simpson, H. Soliman. September 2007. Obsoletes RFC2461.

[132] RFC4862 *IPv6 Stateless Address Autoconfiguration.* S. Thomson, T. Narten, T. Jinmei September 2007. Obsoletes RFC2462.

[133] RFC4864 *Local Network Protection for IPv6* G. Van de Velde, T. Hain, R. Droms, B. Carpenter, E. Klein May 2007

[134] RFC4868 *Using HMAC-SHA-256, HMAC-SHA-384 and HMAC-SHA-512 with IPsec*, S. Kelly and S. Frankel, May 2007.

[135] RFC4869 *Suite B Cryptographic Suites for IPsec*, L.Law, J. Solinas, April 2007.

[136] RFC4877 *Mobile IPv6 Operation with IKEv2 and the Revised IPsec Architecture*. V. Devarapalli, F. Dupont. April 2007

[137] RFC4884 *Extended ICMP to Support Multi-Part Messages*. R. Bonica, D. Gan, D. Tappan, C. Pignataro. April 2007. Updates RFC792, RFC4443, Errata

[138] RFC4891 *Using IPsec to Secure IPv6 in IPv4 Tunnels*, R. Graveman, M. Parthasarathy, P. Savola, H. Tschofenig, May 2007.

[139] RFC4941 *Privacy Extensions for Stateless Address Autoconfiguration in IPv6*. T. Narten, R. Draves, S. Krishnan. September 2007.

[140] RFC4942 *IPv6 Transition/Co-existence Security Considerations* E. Davies, S. Krishnan, P. Savola September 2007

[141] RFC4944 *Transmission of IPv6 Packets over IEEE 802.15.4 Networks* G. Montenegro, N. Kushalnagar, J. Hui, D. Culler September 2007.

[142] RFC4945 *The Internet IP Security PKI Profile of IKEv1/ISAKMP, IKEv2 and PKIX*, B. Korver, August 2007.

[143] RFC4982 *Support for Multiple Hash Algorithms in Cryptographically Generated Addresses (CGAs)*. M. Bagnulo, J. Arkko. July 2007.

[144] RFC4995 *The RObust Header Compression (ROHC) Framework* L-E. Jonsson, G. Pelletier, K. Sandlund July 2007.

[145] RFC4996 *RObust Header Compression (ROHC): A Profile for TCP/IP (ROHC-TCP)* G. Pelletier, K. Sandlund, L-E. Jonsson, M. West July 2007.

[146] RFC5014 *IPv6 Socket API for Source Address Selection*. E. Nordmark, S. Chakrabarti, J. Laganier. September 2007.

[147] RFC5075 *IPv6 Router Advertisement Flags Option*. B. Haberman, Ed., R. Hinden. November 2007

[148] RFC5095 *Deprecation of Type 0 Routing Headers in IPv6*. J. Abley, P. Savola, G. Neville-Neil. December 2007.

[149] RFC5175 *IPv6 Router Advertisement Flags Option*. B. Haberman, Ed., R. Hinden. March 2008.

[150] RFC5114 *Additional Diffie-Hellman Groups for Use with IETF Standards* S. Kent January 2008.

[151] *IPv6 Ready Logo Program*. IPv6 Forum. November 2007.

[152] *DoD IPv6 Standard Profiles For IPv6 Capable Products Version 3.0*, DISR IPv6 Standards Technical Working Group,13 June 2008.

[153] *Department of Defense Internet Protocol Version 6 Generic Test Plan Version 3.0* Defense Information Systems Agency, Joint Interoperability Test Command, Fort Huachuca, Arizona, August 2007.

[154] FIPS-140-2 *Security Requirements for Cryptographic Modules*, U.S. National Institute of Standards and Technology, May 2001.

[155] NIST SP 800-56A *Recommendation for Pair-Wise Key Establishment Schemes Using Discrete Logarithm Cryptography (Revised)*, U.S. National Institute of Standards and Technology, March 2007.

[156] NIST SP 800-57 *Recommendation for Key Management – Part 1: General (Revised)*, U.S. National Institute of Standards and Technology, March 2007.

[157] NIST SP 800-59 *Guideline for Identifying an Information System as A National Security System*, August 2003.

[158] NIST SP 800-94 *Guide to Intrusion Detection and Prevention (IDP) Systems*, K. Scarfone and P. Mell, U.S. National Institute of Standards and Technology, August 2006.

[159] NIST IR-7007 *An Overview of Issues in Testing Intrusion Detection Systems*, U.S. National Institute of Standards and Technology, Internal Report, P. Mell and V. Hu, June 2003.

[160] NIST SP 500-273 *IPv6 Test Methods: General Description and Validation*. To be published.

[161] *Technical and Economic Assessment of Internet Protocol Version 6 (IPv6)*, IPv6 Task Force, U.S. Department of Commerce, January 2006.

[162] *Internet Protocol Version Six Information Assurance Test Plan*, Draft Version 0.1, National Security Agency/I151.

[163] *Firewall Design Considerations for IPv6*, Enterprise Applications Division of the Systems and Network Analysis Center (SNAC) Information Assurance Directorate National Security Agency, Report # I733-041R-2007, October 2007.

[164] *A Filtering Strategy for Mobile IPv6*, Enterprise Applications Division of the Systems and Network Analysis Center (SNAC) Information Assurance Directorate National Security Agency, Report # I733-040R-2007, September 2007.

[165] *The Modular Firewall Certification Criteria*, Baseline Module version 4.1, ICSA Labs, January 2005.

[166] OMB M-05-22 *Transition Planning for Internet Protocol Version 6 (IPv6)*, Office of E-Government and Information Technology, Office of Management and Budget, August 2005.

[167] OMB IPv6 FAQ *Federal Government Transition Internet Protocol Version 4 (IPv4) to Internet Protocol Version 6 (IPv6) – Frequently Asked Questions*. OMB Office of E-Gov and IT.

[168] *Addressing Guidance for Agency IPv6 Adoption*. OMB Office of E-Gov and IT. To be published.

[169] IPv6 Documents, Federal CIO Council.

[170] *IPv6 Transition Guidance*. Federal CIO Council Architecture and Infrastructure Committee. February 2006.

[171] ISO/IEC 17011:2004 *Conformity assessment -- General requirements for accreditation bodies accrediting conformity assessment bodies.*

[172] ISO/IEC 17025:1999 *General requirements for the competence of testing and calibration laboratories.*

[173] ISO/IEC 17050-1:2004 *Conformity assessment -- Supplier's declaration of conformity -- Part 1: General requirements*

[174] ISO/IEC 17050-2:2004 *Conformity assessment -- Supplier's declaration of conformity -- Part 2: Supporting documentation*

[175] IEEE Std 1003.1-2004 *Standard for Information Technology - Portable Operating System Interface (POSIX). Open Group Technical Standard: Base Specifications, Issue 6.*

[176] *ETSI TC MTS-IPT: IPv6 Testing and eEurope Project,* http://www.ipt.etsi.org/.

[177] *Go4IT: Advanced Tools and Services for IPv6 Testing,* http://www.go4-it.eu/.

[178] *THAI Project, Test and Verification for IPv6,* http://www.tahi.org/.

Appendix C— Terms

Authentication: The process of determining whether some entity is who or what it is declared to be.

Autonomous System: A collection of IP networks and routers under the control of one entity, that presents a common routing policy to the Internet, and as further defined in RFC 1930.

Conformance Testing: Testing to determine if a device satisfies the criteria specified in a controlling document, such as an RFC.

DISR: DoD Information Technology Standards Registry.

Dual-Stack: An Internet Node capable of communicating using either or both of IPv4 and IPv6.

Encryption: The process of translating a *plaintext* message into an encoded *ciphertext* message, usually accomplished using a secret key and a cryptographic cipher.

Exterior Routing: Routing IP packets between Administrative Domains, or Autonomous Systems. Commonly achieved with a protocol such as the Border Gateway Protocol (BGP).

Firewall: A device that acts as a barrier to prevent unauthorized or unwanted communications between sections of a computer network.

Header: That portion at the beginning of a packet containing the information specific to a given protocol.

Host: Any node that is not a Router. In general this profile is limited to discussions of general purpose computers, and not highly specialized devices.

Integrity: Whether the transmitted information is reliable and can be trusted.

Interoperability Testing: Testing to ensure that two or more communications devices can interwork and exchange data.

IPv4 Address: The 32 bit address of a device, for nodes that communicate using the IPv4 protocol.

IPv6 Address: The 128 bit address of a device, for Nodes that communicate using the IPv6 protocol.

Interior Routing: Routing IP packets within a single Administrative Domain, or Autonomous System. Commonly achieved with a protocol such as OSPF or RIP.

Multicasting: The transmission of an IP packet to a "host group", a set of zero or more hosts identified by a single IP destination address.

Network Protection Device: A device such as a Firewall or Intrusion Detection device that selectively blocks packet traffic based on configurable and emergent criteria.

Packet Forwarding: The degenerate case of Routing where only a single outgoing link is available to forward the packet (different from the incoming link).

Performance Testing: Testing to evaluate the compliance of a device to specified performance requirements.

PRF: Pseudo Random Function.

RFC: Request for Comments. A publication of the Internet Engineering Task Force (IETF). The basic Internet specifications are published as RFCs.

Router: a Node that interconnects subnetworks by packet forwarding.

Tunnel: Two endpoints that communicate using an IP packet header or address space, through a network which uses another packet header or address space. This is usually achieved by encapsulating an IP packet (v4 or v6) within another IP packet (v4 or v6).

USG: The United States Government, comprising the Federal Agencies.

www.ingramcontent.com/pod-product-compliance
Lightning Source LLC
Chambersburg PA
CBHW080600060326
40689CB00021B/4895